LARGE PRINT

WOMEN OF THE BIBLE FOR

© 2024 BY URBAN SPIRIT, LLC. ALL RIGHTS RESERVED

No part of this document may be reproduced or transmitted in any form or by any means, electronic, mechanical, photo-copying, or otherwise without prior written permission of Urban Spirit, LLC. All scripture quotations, unless otherwise indicated, are taken from the King James Version Bible.

ISBN: 978-0-9884572-7-0 (Hardcover)

Photo credits: iStock.com

Production: Cheryl Wilson - i4Details

Cover and interior designed by Larry P. Taylor (LTD^2)

*To Beverly, Edna, Olive, Sara and Marianne
thanks for teaching us about true sisterhood
and the love of Christ!*

M

Women of the Bible

THE OLD TESTAMENT

Eve: The First African Woman 11

Hagar: Battered, Beaten and Rejected but Not Abandoned 14

Lot's Wife: Why Look Back? 18

Sarah: Is Anything Too Hard for God 23

Rebekah: A Woman of Obsessive Love 26

Rachel: Taking Care of Business 30

Leah: Courage, Resistance and Struggle 32

Dinah: An Abused Woman 34

Tamar: A Violated Woman 36

Jochebed: She Knew It Would Take a Village 38

Zipporah: Fulfilling Her Purpose 41

Miriam: Plagued by Jealousy 45

Zelophad's Daughters: Seeking an Inheritance 49

Rahab: Willing to Be Used by God 53

Ascah: A Wise Daughter 56

Deborah: An Uncommon Leader 60

Jael: Just Another Woman on the Lord's Side 62

The Woman of Thebez: Protector of Her People 64

Samson's Mother: The Strength of a Wife and Mother 66

Samson's Bride: Nothing by Chance 68

Delilah: Strength that Builds or Destroys 70

Micah's Mother: The Consequence of Ignoring God 74

The Levite's Concubine: Broken Pieces 79

Naomi: Call Me Bitter 82

Ruth: A Model of Friendship and Sisterhood 86
Hannah: What Do You Do When God Say's "No"? 90
Michal: A Disappointed Bride 92
Abigail: A Wise Wife 94
Bathsheba: A Silent Affair 96
Tamar: The Link Between Judah and Jesus 98
Rizpah: A Grieving Mother 100
The Queen of Sheba: In Search of True Wisdom 105
The Prophet's Widow: God Provides 108
The Shunammite Woman: Our Sister's Grief is Our Grief 113
Jezebel: A Wicked Queen 116
Huldah: A Prophetess of God 120
Jehosheba: Standing Firm 122
Athaliah: An Angry Woman 124
Queen Vashti: A Woman of Strength 126
Esther: More than a Beauty Queen 128
Job's Wife: She Was Tested Too 131
Wisdom Personified: The Cry of Wisdom 135
The Adulteress of Proverbs: The Path to Death 138
A Virtuous Woman: A Strong Woman Dependent on God 142
The Bridegroom and His Bride: Soul Mates in Life 146
Ezekiel's Wife: On God's Stage 150
Gomer: An Unfaithful Wife 152

THE NEW TESTAMENT

The Canaanite Woman: Persistence Pays Off 156
Wise and Foolish Virgins: Preparing for Christ 158
Mary Magdalene: Setting Her Reputation Straight 160

Daughter of Jarius: A Testament of Faith 162

Herodias and Salome: Evil Choices 166

The Widow's Offering: Selfless Giving 170

The Servant Girl: The Truth, the Whole Truth and Nothing but the Truth 175

Mary, the Mother of James and Joseph: Sacrificing for Christ 178

Mary, the Mother of Jesus: A Model of Motherhood............ 182

Anna: A Model of Spiritual Devotion........................... 184

Peter's Mother-In-Law: From Suffering to Service.............. 186

Hemorrhaging Woman: Faith to Press In 188

The Persistent Widow: Always Pray 190

The Forgiven Adulteress: Caught but Not Condemned 193

Mary and Martha: Grieving Sisters 196

Mary of Bethany: The Unforgotten Woman..................... 200

Sapphira: A Lost Opportunity for Truth 205

Candace: Secure Leader 208

Rhoda: Doing Her Duty 210

Lydia: A Model for Women in Business......................... 212

Fortune-Telling Slave Girl: A Surprising Testimony to God's Work... 214

Philip's Daughters: Those Preachin Women 216

Phoebe: A Faithful Messenger 219

Priscilla: An Open-Door Policy................................. 223

Euodia and Syntyche: Women in Conflict 226

Claudia: A Sincere Supporter 230

The "Chosen Lady": A Woman Worth Imitating................. 234

The Revelation 12 Woman: A Woman of Focus 239

Old Testament

EVE

The First African Woman

The story of Eve is relevant to women of color for several reasons. It is no secret that women of color have reigned throughout history as the first women to do many things in God's world.

The creation of Eve, the first woman of color, occurred on the sixth day of creation.

In the first chapters of Genesis, the story of the creation of Eve demonstrates the importance of men and women complementing one another, supporting one another and empowering one another.

When women of color develop and nurture relationships—whether intimate, professional, familial or social—we must remember the importance of embracing and empowering through our role as "helper" (Ge 2:20). I define helper not only in the sense of a husband-wife team or a male-female relationship, but also inclusively from a Biblical stance: women helping women, women helping men, women helping children, women helping the community and women helping others who may or may not be like them.

Eve's story also shows the challenge of listening and hearing God when God speaks to us. When we fail to hear God's voice, we move in the wrong direction, and we commit sin. Eve first sinned when she listened to the serpent instead of God (see Ge 3:1–8). There will be times when we listen to the wrong voice, but it's important to remember that we can always go to God and seek forgiveness.

There is no need to hide from God. God wants us to confess our wrongs to him. In fact, in Genesis 3:9 God asked Adam and Eve, "Where are you?" The question

Eve

"Where are we in our relationship to God?" should be ever before us.

The story of Eve should remind women of color that God has created each of us in his image. We know that God has empowered and inspired many women of color to be pioneers, to be helpers and to be women who listen to the voice of God.

— P. Williams

Where are you in your relationship with God? Whose voice are you listening to?

Read: Genesis 1:27; 2:18—4:25; Romans 5:18–19; 2 Corinthians 11:3.

HAGAR

Battered, Beaten and Rejected—but Not Abandoned

Given her story, it's no surprise that women of color find a kindred spirit in the person of Hagar. She was a young slave from Egypt who found herself in the midst of a foreign, nomadic people.

She was forced to give her body to her master, Abram—an idea first proposed by his wife, Sarai (see Ge 16:1–3). But once she obeyed her mistress and master, she was rejected and scorned.

Sarai's mistreatment of the pregnant Hagar forced the young woman to run away. Hagar fled into the desert where she met the angel of God. He told her to return to Sarai and give birth to Abram's son, Ishmael, who would become the father of a nation. Hagar was amazed that the living God saw her. Filled with hope, Hagar returned and gave birth to her son (see Ge 16:4–15).

In God's time and by God's grace, the promised son, Isaac, was born to Sarah and Abraham (see Ge 21:1–7), whose names were changed by God before Isaac's birth. After Isaac's birth Sarah saw Hagar's child as a threat to Isaac's position as heir, so she implored Abraham to expel them (see Ge 21:8–13).

Hagar and Ishmael were sent into the desert with a meager supply of food and water. When the water ran out, Hagar sat apart from her son so as to not witness his death. Again, the angel of God appeared to reassure her of God's plan and to reveal to her a well of drinking water. Refreshed, renewed and redirected, Hagar raised her son alone. Ishmael grew to be a strong, powerful man and founder of the Arab nations (see Ge 21:14–21; 25:13–18).

Disadvantaged and dispossessed women today can relate to Hagar. Many have experienced estrangement, prejudice, hardship, hopelessness, grief and despair. Many have known the fear that accompanies being an abandoned, pregnant woman alone in the world.

Regardless of your circumstances, your social status, or how many times you've been knocked down, battered and beaten by life, you cannot escape God's care. God provided for Hagar and her son, and he can and will provide for you.

—T. Wade

Reflect on a time when you felt battered, beaten and rejected. How did God refresh, renew and redirect you? Consider sharing your testimony with a woman who is experiencing rejection.

Read: Genesis 16; 21; 25:12–18.

LOT'S WIFE

Why Look Back?

We know the story of Lot's wife, who disobeyed God by looking back at the cities of Sodom and Gomorrah and, consequently, turned into a pillar of salt (see Genesis 19:15–26).

Lot, Abraham's nephew, was a man of substance. He had done well in the sinful city of Sodom and was held in some respect. Genesis 19:1 says that Lot was "sitting in the gateway of the city." Such a position would indicate that Lot was probably a member of Sodom's ruling council.

Because of Lot's power and respect, his wife, Mrs. Lot, also received some level of respect in their community. She enjoyed the comforts afforded her because of her relationship with her husband.

Lot's wife is a perfect example of the principle "Where your treasure is, there your heart will be also" (Mt 6:21). When the angels told her family to leave, she started out in the right direction and followed Lot outside the city, yet she was destroyed because she looked back. She was not totally committed to giving up her old ways in obedience to God.

Think about all that we as women/sisters have willingly put up with in those times when we have allowed ourselves to be belittled, put down and mistreated (verbally and physically) just to have a man, a job, material possessions, a certain lifestyle or something else we thought we needed so badly.

Lord, help us! When God releases us from that foolishness and makes a way out of no way, we dare to look back with some regret, some desire for what was—to a moment when things were "good."

Those who put their hand to the gospel plow have no reason to look back now.

—M. Bellinger

Use the story of Lot's wife as a reminder to keep looking forward to all God has in store for you. Do not let your past keep you from moving forward.

Read: Genesis 18–19; Luke 9:62; 17:28–32.

SARAH

Is Anything Too Hard for God?

Sarah was a woman after my own heart; in many ways, she represents women of faith who step out on God's Word—even when they don't understand how things will work out.

When God instructed Abraham to leave his father's household and go to the country of God's choosing, Sarah was 65 years old and Abraham was 75. God promised that he would make Abraham and his descendants a blessing to many. Abraham obeyed God and took Sarah, Lot (his nephew) and all of their possessions and headed for Canaan (see Ge 12:1–5).

God spoke directly to Abraham and indirectly to Sarah. Sarah obeyed God by supporting her husband's plans for the move. It is not said very often, but there are many African American women who love their husbands, move when they say it's time to go, and happily follow their leadership. Many of us are blessed to have strong men who listen to God and obey his Word. The Bible gives wonderful examples of good marriages and provides guidance on how to experience a blessed marriage.

Just like many women of faith—married and single—Sarah began an awesome journey based on God's promises. However, many years passed and Sarah and Abraham still did not have their promised child. Sarah began to believe that she would never have a child of her own for Abraham. So, she persuaded Abraham to take her Egyptian servant girl as a surrogate wife, and Ishmael was born to Hagar (see Ge 16). Both Sarah and Abraham forgot God's ability to fulfill his promises. Sarah's attempt at assisting God had dire consequences for the descendants of Ishmael (Arabs) and Isaac (Israelites/Jews).

Sarah's bitter jealousy and anger toward Hagar destroyed the family unit. "A woman's family is held together by her wisdom, but it can be destroyed by her foolishness" (Pr 14:1, paraphrased). Sister Sarah did mess up, just as we sometimes mess up. But God keeps his promises! At age 90, Sarah became pregnant by Abraham when he was 100 years old (see Ge 21). Is anything too hard for God?

Sarah gave birth to a son, Isaac, through whom all nations have been blessed in the person of the Messiah, our Lord and Savior, Jesus Christ. Sarah's story reminds women of faith that we are not perfect; however, we can trust God's promises as we journey along the path of life. God will deliver—even when we don't understand how.

—B. Yates

Reflect on a time you tried to "assist" God in bringing about his promises, as Sarah did by giving Hagar to Abraham. What were the results? How has this lesson reminded you to wait on God's timing for the fulfillment of his promises?

Read: Genesis 16; 18:1–15; 21:1–7; Hebrews 11:8–12.

Rebekah

A Woman of Obsessive Love

Rebekah was unable to have children for nearly 20 years after marrying Isaac. But Isaac prayed for his wife, and finally Rebekah conceived twin boys—Jacob and Esau (see Ge 25:19–26). Although Esau was the eldest and entitled to his father's inheritance and blessing,

Rebekah favored her younger son, Jacob, and desired that he take the place of Esau as the inheritor. When the opportunity arose, Rebekah helped Jacob deceive his father. Isaac, who had become old, feeble and blind, bestowed upon Jacob the family blessing and inheritance that was intended for Esau (see Ge 27:1–30).

Rebekah later protected Jacob from Esau's wrath by sending him to stay with her brother Laban in Haran. Unfortunately, Rebekah and Jacob were never reunited, and upon her death, Rebekah was buried in the family burial ground at Machpelah.

It is instinctive and proper for a woman—a wife and mother—to love passionately. But Rebekah's love for Jacob became a selfish, jealous love that led to favoritism of one child over another. Her love for Jacob also led her to compromise her love for, and loyalty to, her husband. She was determined to do what she thought would help Jacob, at the expense of both Esau and Isaac.

Unlike Rebekah's case, sometimes we hear that crimes of passion have ultimately led to the deaths of innocent people. As mothers and spouses, we must take care that our love for our children and our spouses does not become an obsessive love—a love that would allow us to succumb to the temptation of Satan, to betray moral ethics, covenant relationships and spiritual commitments. As women of God, our love should always be pure and subject to the Spirit of God.

God's love for us serves as the ultimate, true example of a pure love—a love that is unconditional, shows no bias or favoritism and is not jealous or boastful. Unselfish motives or desires define pure love: It always protects, always trusts, always hopes, always perseveres and, above all, never fails (see 1Co 13:7–8).

—T. Dixon

Evaluate the love you have for family members. How can you make sure your love is pure and subject to God's Spirit?

Read: Genesis 24–27; 1 Corinthians 13.

RACHEL
Taking Care of Business

What was Rachel doing when she met Jacob, the man who fell in love with her? We often hear about how Jacob was smitten with Laban's pretty daughter; we read how he told Laban that he would work seven years for Rachel's hand in marriage; we remember how Jacob served that seven years, and then Laban tricked him and gave him Leah, Rachel's older sister. Because Jacob desired to have Rachel, he worked for Laban another seven years (see Ge 29:16–30). But what made Rachel so attractive that she was worth 14 years of labor? Was it simply her beauty? Or did Jacob see something else in the young woman?

Perhaps Jacob realized that Rachel was a woman who was taking care of business. When Jacob met Rachel, she was not sitting around waiting to be rescued from her single life. Rachel was working. She was taking care of her father's sheep (see Ge 29:6–12). In fact, her future husband rolled away the stone of a well to aid her in her work. Jacob not only looked upon Rachel's physical beauty, but he likely also noted her dedication and commitment to her father's sheep.

Women who are waiting for their future mates should be taking care of their own business; they should not be idly waiting for someone to make their lives complete or happy. No matter what our situation, we need to understand that we are complete in Christ and that true joy comes from our relationship with him. We should be taking care of God's sheep and living out the purposes God has placed in our hearts. Then when our mates come along, they will be willing to help us continue taking care of the business God has given us charge over—they will not want to hinder us.

—K. Washington

How are you living out the purposes God has placed in your life?

Read: Genesis 29:1—30:26; 31:4,14–19,32–35; 33:2,7; 35:16–20.

LEAH
Courage, Resistance and Struggle

Leah's story is one that many women can relate to. It is the story of a woman longing to be loved, looking for validation, yearning to be affirmed. Women who recognize they're on a dead-end road and who therefore desire to know what to do next and how to find a new way can learn from Leah's experiences.

"Leah girl" came to my church last Sunday with her six children. She was tall and lanky and had pretty eyes, but no other feature distinguished her from most "sistas." A member invited "Leah girl" because "Leah girl" had been drawn by her testimony. While on her post as a security guard, "Leah girl" overheard the lament of another young woman. This young woman had been dissed by her man again. Their relationship was a series of broken promises. "Leah girl" walked up and said, "Excuse me, it sounds like you're where I just left."

"Leah girl" had just found the courage to break free from the married man with whom she'd been involved. I bet the first five of her children are named, "This

Leah

time he'll love me." I get the feeling, however, that the youngest is named, "Now I will praise the Lord."

"Leah girl" came to my church last Sunday. She was hungry, thirsty and looking for a relationship with the Lord. She had come to terms with the fact that validation, affirmation and confirmation are gifts from the Lord and not empty promises from immoral brothers. "Leah girl" lifted her face to praise God.

"Leah girl" represents thousands of women looking for love in all the wrong places. The Biblical Leah spent many years competing for Jacob's love, but one day she decided to look to the Lord instead. For many years Leah struggled to feel fulfilled through her relationship with her husband. During some of those years, she found the strength to rely on the Lord; at other times, she fell victim to the trap of looking for validation through another. If your name is "Leah girl," take the first step today to develop a relationship with Christ. Let the Lord create in you that which will bring eternal satisfaction.

—E. Walters

Have you had the courage to leave unhealthy patterns in the past? What got you through? Use your past successes to help break other unhealthy patterns or share your testimony with someone who needs to hear it.

Read: Genesis 29:16–17, 31–35; 30:9–21; 35:23; Ruth 4:11.

DINAH
An Abused Woman

Dinah is a forgotten woman of the Bible. While we know much about her brothers, Jacob's 12 sons, we know very little about this female child, Jacob's only daughter mentioned in Scripture.

Genesis 34 tells the story of Dinah, the daughter of Jacob and Leah. Dinah left the Hebrew campsite to visit the women in the land. Away from the protection of her family enclave, Dinah was taken by Shechem, the son of a local ruler, and raped.

When Jacob learned of his daughter's rape, he was silent. He did not protest against her treatment; instead he listened to the appeals of Dinah's rapist in the interest of political harmony between the Hebrews and the Hivites. While Jacob continued to negotiate, Dinah's brothers began plotting against the Hivites; meanwhile, Dinah was noticeably absent from the proceedings. According to the story, her feelings and views were never taken into consideration. And not until verse 26 does the reader learn that Dinah had been in Shechem's house all along.

As women of color, we may relate to Dinah's story. We may have been devalued simply for being born female in a culture in which male children are granted more prestige and promise. Perhaps we've been abused in the name of love in so-called loving relationships, while those around us ignored our pain. Perhaps family members and friends are fully aware of the abuse but have chosen to turn away in silence.

This chapter tells a tragic story. Is there any redemption here? First, we can relate to the anger of Dinah's brothers when they learned of her rape. They declared that the rape should not have been done (see Ge 34:7). They declared that a violation of one woman is an affront to the entire community. And while their methods of revenge are abhorrent to us, they ultimately removed Dinah from her place of violation. We need to have the same anger as Dinah's brothers had when we hear of violence toward our abused sisters. We, too, can declare that physical and mental abuse are unacceptable and offend the entire community. We must not be silent!

—M. Coleman

When have you seen another woman mistreated? When have you experienced abuse? How can you take action against the wrongs done to you and your sisters?

Read: Genesis 34.

Tamar
The Link Between Judah and Jesus

Tamar is a forgotten heroine in the Bible. Tamar's story begins with the loss of two husbands, Er and Onan (see Ge 38:6–10), sons of Judah. Childless, her future was questionable. Tamar had two choices: (1) she could accept her lot in life; or (2) she could take action. Tamar made the second choice and became her own advocate.

Bound by what was known as "levirate law" to either marry another son of Judah or be liberated by Judah to marry another man, Tamar used her femininity and played on his manliness, dressing as a prostitute (see Ge 38:13–15). Her goal was security by any means necessary, even a pregnancy when she was unmarried. And, though she risked death if found guilty of adultery, she acquired Judah's personal pledge by obtaining his seal, cord and staff as proof of his participation in this sexually immoral act. Not only did Judah's personal items implicate him, they forced him to fulfill his responsibility to her as the father of her child. When Judah realized that he had denied her justice under levirate law, he could only say, "She is more righteous than I" (Ge 38:26).

Tamar gave birth to twins, Perez and Zerah (see Ge 38:27–30). Critics may ask, "Why is this story found in the middle of Joseph's story?" One reason is that it prepares us for Genesis 49, a chapter in which Jacob blesses Judah, his fourth son, with his scepter, a symbol of birthright and kingship traditionally given to the firstborn. The immoral and violent behavior of his three older brothers (Reuben, Simeon and Levi) set the stage for this blessing to be passed to Judah. Thus, it was through the "Lion of Judah" that the house of David was established. David's ancestry is traced back to Perez, one of the twins fathered by Judah through his daughter-in-law Tamar (see Ru 4:18–22; Mt 1:1–3). Here we have the link between Judah and Jesus.

God works in amazing ways. Despite Tamar and Judah's immoral acts, God sovereignly worked out his good plan. No human frailty can thwart his purposes.

—K. Johnson

How has God used one of your so-called mistakes to accomplish his purpose in your life or in the lives of others? Share your testimony with a sister who is beating herself up about one of her mistakes.

Read: Genesis 38; Deuteronomy 25:5–6.

Jochebed
She Knew It Would Take a Village

Somehow Jochebed knew it would take a village not only to raise her child, but also to save his life. So, she started calling on that village from the day of his birth.

The first two village members introduced in the story are midwives named Shiphrah and Puah, who were ordered to kill all male babies born to Hebrew women. But these midwives lied to the king in order to spare the babies' lives (see Ex 1:15–19). Their refusal to kill the male babies was the first step in saving Moses, Jochebed's son.

Jochebed herself performed the second step by managing to conceal her baby for three months, defying the order to throw him into the Nile River. During that time, she carefully constructed a basket of papyrus and coated it with tar and pitch for waterproofing (see Ex 2:3); she observed the bathing patterns of Pharaoh's daughter, the princess; and she coached her daughter, Miriam (another village member), so she would know what to say and do when the princess found the baby. Jochebed also knew that Miriam fully grasped the plan and understood how to suddenly appear and suggest the appropriate nurse for the discovered child.

JOCHEBED

The next step involved an unsuspecting village member: Pharaoh's daughter. She discovered the beautiful baby who had cried at just the right moment and, at Miriam's prompting, the princess hired Jochebed to take care of the child. The princess raised this Hebrew boy in luxury as her own son, naming him Moses.

Yes, Jochebed knew that it would take a village to raise her child, and she used that village well. She was a loving, caring, concerned, resourceful, determined mother. And she was faithful. God heard her prayers and intervened on her behalf. He honored her steadfast purpose by using all her children—Aaron, Miriam and Moses—to lead his people out of bondage.

Jochebed was a woman of courage who feared only God, not people. She had an unwavering faith in God's promises. She teaches us that it doesn't matter who we are or what our circumstances are; it's how we deal with the lumps and bumps—the challenges and responsibilities that come with being a woman and a mother—that really matters.

—M. Kimbrough

Think about the lumps and bumps—the challenges and responsibilities—that stand before you in this season of your life. How can Jochebed's faith and works inspire you to handle your situation?

Read: Exodus 1:8—2:10; Numbers 26:59; Hebrews 11:23–29.

ZIPPORAH

Fulfilling Her Purpose

The African American woman of today has the potential to carry out the purpose for which she was created. It is not necessary that she live in the shadow of another person in order to establish a spiritual legacy.

Historically, many women have faded into the background of stories, unnamed and unnoticed. Often, tradition and culture dictated that a woman's identity be connected to someone else. Such was the case for Zipporah, the daughter of Jethro and the wife of Moses. We can only surmise about her character from the few times she is mentioned and the one time she is quoted (see Ex 2:15–22; 4:24–26; 18:1–6).

Zipporah is introduced as one of seven daughters, possibly the oldest, of the Midianite priest Jethro (also known as Reuel). Moses met this family after fleeing from Egypt. As shepherds, Jethro's daughters courageously faced daily harassment by other shepherds when watering their father's flocks. Moses helped them, and their father repaid him with hospitality and, eventually, with permission to marry Zipporah.

As the wife of Moses and mother of Gershom and Eliezer, Zipporah did not share the same spiritual heritage as her husband. Perhaps this is the reason that the sacred tradition of circumcision had been neglected. While Moses was returning to Egypt, God "was about to kill him," and his life was spared only after one of the boys was circumcised (Ex 4:24–25).

A wife's resistance to God's will not only endangers God's divine purpose for the couple's lives, but it also places her family in spiritual jeopardy. Zipporah's action and her words of reproach to Moses lead us to assume that her sons likely remained uncircumcised due to her prejudice against a rite not practiced among her people. However, her actions saved her husband's life. She gave in to what she apparently came to realize was the will of God, which brought about a positive result from a frightening situation.

Women of color must be like Zipporah and follow God's will—when we agree and when we do not. We must remember that we see only a portion; God sees the entire picture and knows what is best for us.

—A. Aubry

What is God asking you to do that you do not agree with? How will you submit to the will of God?

Read: Exodus 2:15–22; 4:18–26; 18:2–6.

Miriam

Plagued by Jealousy

Miriam was the daughter of Amram and Jochebed, and the sister of Aaron and Moses. Bible scholars assume her to be the sister mentioned in Exodus 2 who watched the basket that held baby Moses float through the reeds to the pharaoh's palace.

Miriam watched from afar as Pharaoh's daughter retrieved the basket and claimed Moses as her son. Miriam offered to get a wet nurse—the child's own mother, unbeknownst to Pharaoh's daughter (see Ex 2:7–9).

Years later, Moses fled Egypt and settled in Midian. He met Zipporah, the daughter of Jethro, a Midianite priest, and married her (see Ex 2:15–21). Sometime later, Miriam and Aaron criticized Moses "because of his Cushite wife" (Nu 12:1). We are not certain if Zipporah is to be identified as this woman that Miriam and Aaron spoke against. It is possible (though not necessarily so) that the Cushite wife mentioned here was another woman Moses had married.

In addition to their criticisms related to Moses' wife, Miriam and Aaron questioned and challenged Moses' sole right to speak for God to the people. As a result of opposing Moses—which stemmed from jealousy— Miriam was stricken with leprosy (see Nu 12:9–10). After Moses and Aaron interceded with God on Miriam's behalf, she was healed of her leprosy after a seven-day confinement (see Nu 12:11–15).

The spirit of Miriam is alive and well in many women today. We daily suffer physical and spiritual calamities as a result of the deeply rooted jealousies that we harbor. It is jealousy that creates criticism and envy of our friends, loved ones and even strangers. Jealousy and the actions that result from it are not of God.

So then, how do we thwart or control jealousy? How do we prevent ourselves from suffering Miriam's plight? We must be "reborn" each day, seeking God in our every thought and action. We need to pray to him for strength to be Spirit-minded, Christ-centered and God-directed in our homes, workplaces, communities and, most of all, in our churches.

—T. Dixon

Do you sometimes struggle with jealousy and criticism? Ask God to receive glory from your life as he deals with you.

Read: Exodus 2:4–10; 15:20–21; Numbers 12:1–16; 20:1; 26:59; Deuteronomy 24:9; Micah 6:4.

Zelophad's Daughters

Seeking an Inheritance

The Bible speaks of daughters as well as sons; however, the daughters often appear in the background. The genealogies go on and on as they list the sons, but what about the daughters?

We find one powerful account of daughters in Numbers 27—the daughters of Zelophehad. The Biblical account relates how they courageously requested to receive a family inheritance in anticipation of the Israelites' entrance into the promised land. The tradition was that land allotments remained in the family through a male relative, thus perpetuating the ancestral name. Zelophehad's daughters made a request that not only challenged that tradition but also changed the laws of the community. Their actions were personal, yet the results brought about change in the legal and cultural system by becoming case law.

The five daughters—Mahlah, Noah, Hoglah, Milcah and Tirzah—were amazing women. Because their father had died in the desert leaving no male heir, they realized that his name and their family's portion in Canaan would be lost. They were not trying to be aggressive and annihilate the values and norms of their culture, but they did want to be heard. So, they took a risk and made their claim within the context of their religious, cultural and legal system. They put themselves in a position of being rebuffed or blessed. Because they boldly presented a legitimate request, they were blessed, and so, too, were many who came behind them.

The inheritance given to Mahlah, Noah, Hoglah, Milcah and Tirzah demonstrates that God does not give women secondary status and that he is concerned for them. These sisters were rewarded for their faith in God and in his justice for their welfare and personal security. They asked and they received. Often we receive not because we ask not!

The story of Zelophehad's daughters in Numbers 27:1–11 provides the following lesson for women today: Proclaim who you are and that you have God-given rights. Know how your culture constrains or supports you as you claim your rights, and know that asserting yourself can lead to changes in your society that will benefit future generations.

—B. McRipley

What lessons do you learn from Zelophehad's daughters? How can you use these lessons to inspire you and motivate your sisters around you?

Read: Numbers 27:1–11; 36:1–12.

RAHAB

Willing to Be Used by God

Rahab's story shows that God can use anyone. Rahab was a prostitute whose house was part of Jericho's defensive wall.

When Joshua sent spies into Jericho, the spies lodged in Rahab's house (see Jos 2:1). When the king of Jericho sent soldiers in search of the spies, Rahab courageously hid them on the rooftop and told the king's soldiers that the spies were not there (see Jos 2:2–6). Because of her great courage and kindness, the spies promised Rahab that her family would not be harmed during the destruction of Jericho.

Just before Rahab helped the spies escape safely through a window, they instructed her to hang a scarlet cord from her window so that the Israelites would be able to identify the family that should be spared (see Jos 2:14–18). Rahab told the spies that she had heard stories about God's miracles and that she recognized their God as the one true God (see Jos 2:8–11).

Rahab's story has taught women throughout time that God uses whomever he chooses to fulfill his mission. God doesn't always choose the most righteous; he chooses those who are the most willing.

Rahab's belief in God gave her the courage to help the spies. The greater news, however, is that in spite of the fact that she was a prostitute, God chose her to assist Joshua in his mission to capture Jericho. Her faith earned her a place in the "Hebrews Hall of Faith" (see Heb 11:31) and a listing in the genealogy of Jesus (see Mt 1:5).

When God comes into our hearts, we can truly become new people. However, we must remain faithful in reaching for the courage and boldness that allows us to take the first steps toward him. And as women of God, we must remember to not discount others who do not act as we do. They, too, may be used by God and can become new creations.

—T. Dixon

What is God's plan for you this day? How has God used you in spite of yourself to accomplish his will?

Read: Joshua 1:2,11; 2:1–24; Matthew 1:5; Hebrews 11:31; James 2:25.

ACSAH

A Wise Daughter

Although she is a little-known woman of the Bible, Acsah is a wonderful role model for women today. She used her wisdom and knowledge to provide for her family.

The story of Acsah is found in the books of Joshua and Judges. Acsah was the daughter of Caleb, who achieved fame as one of the two spies of Israel who gave a good report about the promised land (see Nu 13:26–33). Later, we read that at the age of 85, Caleb reminded Joshua of the promise that had been given him by Moses regarding the land of Canaan (see Jos 14:6–15). Caleb had success in driving out some of the inhabitants of the land that he acquired; however, he needed help to conquer the land of Debir. In order to do this, he offered his daughter Acsah in marriage as an incentive (see Jos 15:13–17).

The account of Acsah implies she and Caleb enjoyed a close relationship. Although she was used as a commodity to help her father conquer land, Acsah used her wisdom to make the best of her situation. The Negev, the southern part of Judah, is a hot, dry region with less than eight inches of rainfall annually. Water is a necessity, and springs make life easier in this harsh country. The wording of Acsah's request suggests that she had some knowledge of what life was like in this area. She was wise enough to get her husband's consent before asking her father to give her a dowry of commercial value and productivity (see Jos 15:18–19).

The exchange between Caleb and his nephew Othniel is unknown; however, Caleb respected his daughter enough to want to know her wishes. Acsah's story is an account of an obedient daughter who did not bemoan her fate but utilized wisdom. Her actions possibly allowed her family to become successful and respected in the community, for we later learn that Othniel became the first judge of Israel after Joshua's death (see Jdg 3:9–11).

—M. Copeland

Reflect on a time you used wisdom to make the best of a seemingly bad situation. How does that past experience inspire you to use wisdom in a situation you are dealing with today?

Read: Joshua 15:13–19; Judges 1:11–15; 3:9–11.

Deborah
An Uncommon Leader

Deborah—a strong, courageous leader—serves as a great example for women of color today. Like many women, Deborah lived during a time when there was much unrest in her nation (see Jdg 4:1). Deborah served as a judge and prophetess during Israel's bondage under Jabin, a king of Canaan, who resided in Hazor. Sisera, the captain of Jabin's army, was renowned for having 900 iron chariots. He was also known for his oppression of the Israelites (see Jdg 4:2–3).

Deborah's name means "bee," which is very appropriate. She gathered the people to her as honey, but her sting was most fatal to her enemies. She was a godly woman who wore many hats—that of prophet, poet, encourager, warrior, wife and ruler.

God chose Deborah to minister justice and to lead his people out of bondage into peace. Deborah was one of several women distinguished in Scripture by her ability to discern the purposes of God. When God spoke to her, she took action.

DEBORAH

God directed Deborah to speak to one who could deliver the Israelites from their enemies. Deborah sent for Barak, the son of Abinoam, and related the instructions God had for him and the promise of victory if he obeyed. Barak replied that he would lead their army to war only if Deborah would go with him; if she would not go, he would not go. Deborah agreed to go, but she informed Barak that the victory would now be credited to a woman (see Jdg 4:6–10).

It all happened as Deborah said. God delivered Sisera into the hands of Jael, who killed him with a tent peg (see Jdg 4:21). And God rescued the Israelites from their foes. Because of Deborah's obedience and willingness to act, she is remembered today for her leadership and courage.

—J. Fosey

How can Deborah's story inspire you to live up to being the woman God has called you to be?

Read: Judges 4–5.

JAEL
Just Another Woman on the Lord's Side

Jael is clearly a true role model for women of color today—she used what was at her disposal to accomplish what she understood to be her fight.

We don't know much about this woman whose account is found in the book of Judges. We don't know whose daughter she was. She is simply described as the wife of Heber the Kenite. Many years earlier, Moses had married a Kenite woman, and a number of these nomadic people later settled among the Israelites in the promised land (see Jdg 1:16).

Though the Kenites were long-time allies of Israel, Heber was on the side of the enemy. Most likely he told Sisera, the commander of the enemy army, where Israel's army was camped (see Jdg 4:12). Jael, however, had her own thoughts about the matter.

Jael may or may not have known Israel's God. Nevertheless, the sequence of events suggests that Jael knew enough to know that being on the Lord's side was the better choice.

JAEL

When Israel's victory was certain, Sisera ran for his life to his friend's home. Jael invited him in. She gave the exhausted soldier something to drink and then covered him up. When he fell asleep, Jael took a hammer and used it to drive a tent peg through his skull, killing him instantly.

Although we don't know much about Jael and her motives, we know enough to celebrate this woman of great courage. She was obviously a woman of deep conviction. She had the big picture in view. She realized that helping Israel was the right thing to do.

Womanhood was honored as Deborah and Jael were used by God to accomplish his purpose of delivering his people from their enemies. Although Jael's actions fulfilled Deborah's prophecy, she may have known only that Israel was on the Lord's side. But that was enough.

There are times in a woman's life when she must take a stand. It may mean risking your career, social status or something else more precious. Life will present you with many battles and many decisions, so choose carefully. Never go into battle unless you are on the Lord's side. Never fight for the sake of personal glory. Be certain that your motivation is the liberation and redemption of God's people.

—E. Walters

What have you taken a stand for in life? What have you had to sacrifice? How has God received the glory?

Read: Judges 4:11–24; 5:24–27.

The Woman of Thebez

Protector of Her People

She is a nameless woman. Scripture gives no clue concerning her parentage. We only know her as the anonymous woman who killed Abimelech, one of the sons of Gideon, by throwing a millstone from the tower of Thebez (see Jdg 9:52–54).

The people of Thebez were under siege by Abimelech and his men (see Jdg 9:50–51). The people had fled to the tower for safety. Abimelech followed them, intending to set the tower on fire. As he approached the tower, a woman dropped a "millstone on his head and cracked his skull" (Jdg 9:53). Since grinding grain was considered "women's work" during this period, we can see that the woman used what she had on hand—a millstone—to defeat her enemy.

What can we learn from this woman? Obviously, she was a woman who could assess the situation at hand, make a decision and act on that decision with haste. Her immediate response in that moment saved not only her life but also the lives of all those who sought refuge in the tower. Surely the woman understood that in her culture it was unlikely that she would receive any credit for her heroism. God used this unnamed woman to perform a small yet significant act (see Jdg 9:56).

How willing are you to step forward when called upon—without worrying about what's in it for you? Each of us should be willing at any given moment to respond when a situation arises in which God is directing us through the Holy Spirit. God knows the motives of our hearts and will reward us for acts that reflect his glory. God called and the woman responded. This is a reminder to each of us to always be ready when God calls us, no matter what the task. God equips us for every task we are sent to do. All we need to do is be a willing vessel.

—J. Hopkins

How willing are you to perform both little and big tasks for God? Be open to opportunities throughout this day.

Read: Judges 9; 2 Samuel 11:21.

SAMSON'S MOTHER
The Strength of a Wife and Mother

The angel of God appeared to an unnamed woman (see Jdg 13). She was Manoah's wife and soon to be Samson's mother. Though her namelessness might imply that she was insignificant, the angel spoke to the woman and revealed that the Lord would use her to give birth to one who would begin to deliver Israel from the Philistines.

Manoah's wife did not address the angel. Instead she told her husband what the Lord had revealed. The angel appeared to the woman a second time. Although Manoah prayed that the divine messenger would return and give further instructions, God did not send the angel directly to him. Why? We could make a couple assumptions here: (1) God speaks to women who will share with their husbands the plans of God; and (2) women are encouraged to carry the story of God's plan of salvation to others. (In Matthew 28:10, Jesus told the women to "go and tell.")

Samson's Mother

Manoah's wife was not a woman who aggressively tried to be her own boss. She heard God. She believed God. She led her husband to the angel of God. She willingly kept quiet while her husband questioned the angel. The angel replied, "Your wife must do all that I have told her" (Jdg 13:13). The responsibility was placed on the woman to do God's bidding.

As the vessel to bring forth deliverance for Israel, she was to refrain from certain things while carrying Israel's liberator. She was not to drink alcohol or eat any unclean food. She was told how to nurture the life of this consecrated child. No razor was to come upon her son's head. He was to be set apart and raised to be used for God's purpose. The child, Samson, would bring destruction to those who hated Israel (see Jdg 13:4–7,13–14).

One of the mysteries of people of color has been their ability to survive the hardships of life and still maintain strength of body and mind. The strength of our women has consistently been faith in God. Samson's mother reminds us to listen to God's instructions and obey him. Those who know their purpose can be great weapons against the enemies of God.

—D. Shumake

How has your faith given you strength? Share your story with a woman who needs strength today.

Read: Judges 13.

Samson's Bride
Nothing by Chance

It is not by chance that Samson's marriage is the first recorded event of his adult life. Samson's bride is first mentioned in Judges 14:1–3. Interestingly, she is not described in the usual patriarchal Biblical tradition as "the daughter of . . ."; instead she is called "a Philistine woman in Timnah" (Jdg 14:2). She is characterized by the place she lived and, more significantly, by her ethnic background. As a Gentile woman, she was a poor choice for a wife for Samson (see Dt 7:3–4). The marriage was doomed from the beginning. Her loyalty to her past ultimately affected her future.

Samson's bride manipulated him into telling her the secret of a riddle he had presented at their wedding banquet. At the demands of her countrymen and their threats of death, she betrayed Samson. Out of vengeance Samson attacked some of the Philistines, while his wife was given to another (see Jdg 14:19–20). Unfortunately, the sad saga did not end there. After Samson exacted his revenge against the Philistines, his wife and her father were murdered. More deaths followed (see Jdg 15:6–8).

The key to understanding this little-known woman is to look at who brought her into Samson's life. The astonishing thing about this story is that God allowed Samson's relationship with this Philistine woman. Judges 14:4 states that "[Samson's] parents did not know that this was from the Lord." Thus, God was orchestrating the circumstances so that Samson—in spite of, and even through, his sinful and impulsive choices—could confront the Philistines and deliver Israel from them.

How reassuring it is to know that even when we, like the woman of Timnah, don't know what God is doing, his sovereign hand still controls the action. Others may not be able to see God in the situation, but we can be assured that God can use any situation. The Philistine woman's presence in Samson's life provided a turning point for him.

We need to recognize that God has placed us in a position of influence as Christian mothers, daughters, wives, sisters, friends and coworkers. As Christians, we must lead lives strengthened by prayer and enhanced by the Word of God. Though we may not see how God is using us, we can know that wherever God has placed us, we are making a difference.

—S. Riley

Reflect on a time when God got the glory from even one of your bad decisions. Walk in this day remembering that God is sovereign.

Read: Judges 14:1—15:8.

Delila

Strength That Builds or Destroys

The story of Samson and Delilah often generates reflection on the weaknesses of Samson. Many questions arise regarding how Samson could be so clueless about Delilah's agenda to assist the

Philistines in his demise. But the story of Samson and Delilah is not necessarily that simple. Delilah has a message for all women to take to heart. Delilah, as many women in the Bible, reminds us of the unusual strength women have—a strength that can either build up or destroy those around us. While women are naturally the weaker sex physically, we possess an exceptional, yet subtle, spiritual and emotional strength.

It is important for women to be conscious of this strength because of its potential to either build up or destroy. Women have the power to build up individuals, families, communities and churches. Likewise, that same power can also destroy. Delilah chose to destroy a man for money. She could have chosen to help build up his character, as Deborah attempted to do with Barak (see Jdg 4:6–7). Instead, as a result of her decision, at the same time that Samson was destroyed, so were thousands of Delilah's people (see Jdg 16:26–30).

Delilah held a special power over Samson's heart— and it wasn't exclusively the power of sexual attraction. Although Delilah had proved herself untrustworthy, she still was able to make Samson feel comfortable with her. The people in our lives—especially our loved ones— need to feel comfortable around us; they need to feel as if they can trust us. We, in turn, should not use this special power to destroy them but to help them grow into the people God has called them to become. Women must be aware of the strength that God has given us and understand that Satan desires to use this strength for evil. We must choose how this God-given strength will be used—to build up or to destroy.

—B. Whitaker

How will you use your special power to build up those around you rather than to destroy them?

Read: Judges 16.

Micah's Mother

The Consequences of Ignoring God

Little is known of the mother of this man named Micah (not the Micah who wrote the book of the Old Testament bearing his name)

except what is written in Judges 17. She lived with her son in Ephraim.

From her story, women of color who are mothers can learn three things that they should not do:

1. Be dishonest. Dishonesty leads to negative consequences. When her son returned 1,100 shekels of silver that he had stolen from her, she stated her intention to consecrate the silver to the Lord in order to counteract the curse that she had cast. She announced that she would give the money back to Micah to make a carved image and a cast idol. She then proceeded to contribute only 200 shekels of silver—a small fraction of her initial promise—for the project (see Jdg 17:4).

2. Disobey the commandments. By encouraging and participating with her son in making idols, she broke one of God's commandments: "You shall not make for yourself an idol in the form of anything" (Ex 20:4).

3. Ignore your family's sinfulness. In addition to participating in the making of idols, there is no indication that Micah's mother tried to stop her son from installing her grandson, and later a Levite who was not a member of the priestly line, as priest. There were rules by which priests were to be chosen, and she and her family ignored God's law. Consequently, her son's actions contributed to his—and Israel's—religious confusion.

We are charged to obey God's commandments in all areas of our lives and to teach—by our words and actions—our families to do the same.

—A. Dise

How do you show those around you that you trust and obey God?

Read: Judges 17.

The Levite's Concubine

Broken Pieces

Judges 19 relates the horrific account of a woman's life and death in such graphic detail that it could cause us to think we're reading a grisly novel rather than the Bible.

This anonymous woman was the concubine (a legitimate, but secondary, wife) of a Levite. After being unfaithful to the Levite, she left him and returned to her father's home. Four months later her husband set out on a journey to convince her to come back to him.

The Levite arrived at the home of his concubine's father. There he spent many days conversing with her father, and he repeatedly put off his journey home in order to stay with his host. Like Lot in Genesis 19, the Levite hesitated (see Ge 19:16). His lack of strength of mind set the stage for the ensuing tragedy.

Finally, the Levite began the journey home, accompanied by his concubine. We do not know if she was coerced or convinced to go, but she left with the Levite and his servant. When evening came, the travelers stopped in an Israelite town in the territory of Benjamin to find shelter for the night. They were taken in by a hospitable stranger just as it began to look as if they would have to spend the night in the town square.

Again, in a story that contains many parallels to that of Lot and Sodom and Gomorrah, men from the town swarmed to the man's door seeking to have sex with the Levite guest. Instead, the man offered his daughter and the Levite's concubine. At first the wicked men of the city refused the offer, but eventually the Levite sent his concubine out to them. Violation and death resulted. The subsequent dismemberment and distribution of the concubine's body led to civil war in Israel.

There are countless women around us today who are broken into many pieces. They have suffered horrors, violence and abuse. Many of these women darken the doors of our churches and ministries; often they remain anonymous, unheard and unspoken to. They literally are standing at the threshold crying out for help, and we step over them and continue on our own journeys, just as the Levite tried to do (see Jdg 19:27).

If you feel broken and wonder if anyone even knows your name, remember that God knows who you are. When society continues to rob you of your dignity, God is able to take every broken piece of your life and bring about wholeness.

—C. Ward

How has God brought about wholeness in your life? Share your story with someone who is broken. If you have not yet experienced wholeness, seek out a sister who has, and ask her to share her story.

Read: Judges 19.

Naomi

Call Me Bitter

My family left our hometown, Bethlehem, with thoughts of a better life. My husband and I packed up our two sons and moved to the country of Moab because there was a famine in Israel.

We became comfortable in Moab. But one day the unthinkable happened: my husband died. The only thing that helped relieve my grief was the marriages of my sons. Although my daughters-in-law were Moabites rather than Israelites, I grew to love them like daughters.

Then, unbelievably, both of my sons died. I was thrown into the depths of despair; and Ruth, Orpah and I were left alone in an unkind world. At the time I thought, It's funny: while my name means "pleasant," my spirit counters such a lighthearted name. Instead, my spirit says, "Call me bitter."

When I heard that the famine was over in Israel, I decided to return home. I thought that at least my people were there, and I could wait my time out to die. My daughters-in-law begged to return to Bethlehem with me because they were determined not to leave me alone. But what could I offer them? While we were on the journey to Israel, I convinced Orpah to return to her family in Moab. But Ruth refused to go. She was determined to accompany me. I reluctantly allowed her to do so.

When we arrived in Bethlehem, our status as widows meant we had no one to care for us. We had no food, and I was too old to work. When my friends tried to comfort me, all I could say was, "Call me bitter." Now I realize just how God blessed me by giving me Ruth. She gleaned in the fields so that we could eat. And when she was fortunate enough to work on the property of one of my relatives, Boaz, she followed my advice and eventually married this kind man. Ruth and Boaz then took care of me. But my story does not end there. When Ruth had a son, she brought him to me to care for! Call me bitter? No! God has taken my bitterness and given me a garment of praise! I praise him for Ruth because I now know that she is more valuable to me than seven sons!

—C. Belt

Reflect on a time when God took away your bitterness and gave you a spirit of praise. How can your past experience inspire you to continue to trust in the Lord?

Read: Ruth 1–4.

RUTH

A Model of Friendship and Sisterhood

The book of Ruth and the woman Ruth have provided the Biblical canon with a captivating voice that reaches far beyond what the writer of this book may have intended.

This brief account holds more than a sentimental Scriptural reference for a wedding or a life design for single women. This story poignantly highlights many of the issues that African American women struggle with today (e.g., family, security, loss, racism, sexism and survival). Ruth is best known for marrying Boaz and giving birth to Obed, an ancestor of David and, consequently, Jesus. But before she claimed her place in history as "wife" and "mother," she added a unique imprint as "woman" and "sista." In Ruth 1:14, we find this Moabite widow making an unprecedented choice to "cling" (or "cleave," kjv) to her Israelite mother-in-law.

The relationship between Ruth and Naomi bound two women who could have easily chosen to become estranged. After the death of her husband (Naomi's son), Ruth was left with an uncertain future. She could return to her home, but there was no guarantee that her family would embrace her, since she had married an Israelite. The Israelites were long-time antagonists of her people. She could follow her mother-in-law, but there was uncertainty about how she would be received as a foreigner with scorned ethnic roots. Using her courage and strength, Ruth remained with, or "clung" to, Naomi. As a result, they were able to move beyond their given identities as wives and widows and establish different identities as partners and sojourners.

The return of Naomi to Bethlehem was the beginning of a new life for her and Ruth. Ruth worked in the fields of Naomi's relative, Boaz. Following the advice of Naomi, Ruth eventually won the love of Boaz, who bought the estate of Naomi and married Ruth.

This story's gift to us is a message about the value of collaboration, cooperation, friendship, love and trust between two women. At a turning point in her life, Ruth continued a relationship that would become a great blessing for both women. By taking risks and working together, Ruth and Naomi became a model for future generations of love, trust and loyalty.

—K. Mosby

How can you work with other women to bring about change for yourself and for others? Is there anything that stands in the way of your cooperating with other women? Seek God's guidance in dealing with your concern.

Read: Leviticus 25:25; Ruth 1:11–18.

Hannah
What Do You Do When God Says "No"?

We never get used to disappointment. To live the life of an infertile woman is heartbreaking on a monthly basis. Hannah had been infertile for many years. Others scorned her because in her culture having children, especially male children, was a symbol of wholeness. Her husband's other wife, Peninnah, who had children, taunted her. Hannah was made to feel incomplete and inadequate as a wife and as a woman.

Through her situation, Hannah teaches us what to do when our desire does not materialize. She shows us how to handle "no" or "not yet" from God. Though Hannah lived with life's disappointments on a daily basis, she re-emphasizes for us the value of prayer. Hannah continued to go to the tabernacle with her husband, Elkanah, to pray. She continued to worship God even though her prayers went unanswered.

Hannah remained faithful to God when it seemed that God had closed the door to her request for a child. She continued to pray and share her pain and sorrows with him (see 1Sa 1:15–16). Hannah never stopped believing that the God she served was able to help her. She prayed without ceasing and continued to worship the only one who could soothe her soul.

When God did say "yes," Hannah responded with joy and love. And she honored him by offering her son back to him. Hannah realized that her son was a gift from God.

Just because God has said "no" now, he may not mean "no" eternally. Sometimes God has to put things in order before he can say "yes." Perhaps there are people and situations that he must work on before our "yes" can come. And sometimes God's "yes" doesn't look like what we thought we wanted—but even then, honor must be given to the giver of all gifts. When God answers our prayers, we must remember to follow Hannah's model and offer our answered prayer back to God; we must honor God with the people and things he gives us.

—L. White

Have you committed to praying to God for all your needs and wants? Use Hannah as a model for handling your "no" and "not yet" moments.

Read: 1 Samuel 1:1—2:11.

Michal
A Disappointed Bride

The story of Michal has a lot to teach women of color. Michal was the daughter of King Saul, but she was in love with a young former shepherd named David. But there was a problem: Her father feared David and was intensely jealous of him. Saul used his daughter as bait, promising her to David in marriage if he would kill a hundred Philistines as a bride price. Saul hoped that young David would himself be killed; but once again David triumphed, and Michal became his wife.

Michal seemed to truly love her husband, even risking her own life to save David's (see 1Sa 19:11–17). However, she soon discovered that her love was not enough to save a marriage besieged by politics and pressure. She was taken from David and given to another man (see 1Sa 25:44). Michal had to learn to lean on God rather than on the things of life.

All of us think that people, things or situations will make us happy. As young girls, we start off early by chasing after designer clothes, popularity and the right relationship. The list can go on and on. Our desires—for materials goods, degrees, power and prestige, money, and wonderful, perfect relationships—can become our idols. We dream about obtaining them, and some of us will do anything to get the things we want, the things we think will make us happy and fulfilled.

Michal needed to know that the true God wanted a relationship—in a sense, a "marriage"—with her. If she had known this, she would have been able to rejoice with her husband when he celebrated before the Lord (see 2Sa 6:16–22). As women we need to know that God wants an intimate relationship with us. We shouldn't put any of our desires before God.

Women and girls of African ancestry, what is our destiny? Will we ever be truly happy simply by being married or when we get the many other things we desire? Michal can help us answer that question with a resounding "no." We must have our own relationship with God and understand what destiny God would have us fulfill. Then we will be fulfilled women.

—B. Garvin

Does God fulfill you more than any other person or thing?

Read: 1 Samuel 18:17–29; 19:11–17; 25:44; 2 Samuel 3:12–16; 6:12–23.

ABIGAIL
A Wise Wife

The story of Abigail shows women today how to deal with challenges. As Abigail's story proves, following wisdom and goodness eventually yields great results.

When David journeyed through the desert after Samuel's death, he sent greetings to Nabal, the rich husband of Abigail. David asked Nabal for a customary gift for services rendered while David's men were on Nabal's property. Nabal refused in a very insulting manner. His behavior was not very surprising however. Nabal's name means "fool" and he lived up to that name. David took offense and rounded up 400 men to attack Nabal and his household. In the meantime, a servant who had overheard Nabal's remarks warned Abigail of David's intentions. Abigail, being the intuitive, wise, beautiful woman of color that she was, took bread, wine, sheep and other gifts and loaded them on donkeys to forestall David's assault on her household.

When Abigail approached David, she quickly dismounted and fell on her face in submission, accepting the blame for her husband's foolish remarks. Her actions and words showed great respect for this man of God. She depended not only on her reasoning, but also on God's grace. She began to remind David of who he was. She also reminded him that vengeance belongs to the Lord, who is the captain of the battlefield.

David repented and thanked Abigail for being an instrument of God by reminding him not to take matters into his own hands.

Upon returning home, Abigail found her husband drunk after a feast. She was not able to tell him anything about what had transpired earlier that day. When he awoke the next morning, she shared with him the previous day's events. When she confronted him, his heart became as stone. Ten days later "the Lord struck Nabal and he died" (1Sa 25:38).

When David heard that Nabal was dead, he rejoiced in the judgment of God. Because of his regard for Abigail, he sent for her to be his wife. Abigail earned David's respect. She models for women today wisdom and determination to make the best of a bad situation.

—P. George

What situations in your life require wisdom and determination to bring about success? Seek God for guidance.

Read: 1 Samuel 25:1–44; 2 Samuel 3:3.

BATHSHEBA
A Silent Affair

The story of Bathsheba elicits different kinds of responses. It is a story of sin, sorrow, redemption and consequence. It is a story of a powerful man who went after what he wanted and a woman who had little power to resist being used by him. We learn of the humanity of King David, the faithfulness of Uriah and the silence of Bathsheba.

Women of color have experienced ultimate powerlessness. With our history of slavery, we understand oppression and male domination. We understand a culture in which women, especially women of color, are treated like pawns in the larger scheme of political progress and ambition.

In Bathsheba's time, women generally had no voice, no power, no place in decision making. Their voices were rarely heard. In this story, the only time we read that Bathsheba spoke was to send word to King David that she was pregnant (see 2Sa 11:5). We hear nothing more from her for the remainder of the story. Like so many other Biblical women, we don't really know Bathsheba's personal perspective. She may have felt reluctant to be with King David; she may have felt that she could not refuse the king; or she may have been a willing partner. Many things are unknown, but we do know that King David went to great lengths to be with Bathsheba and that he plotted her husband's death after learning that she was pregnant.

In this story, we learn that there are consequences for our behavior, that true prophets of God speak the truth even to the king, that sinful behavior is not acceptable to God, and that God forgives us when we confess our sins. Read the story of David and Bathsheba with the knowledge that God loves the people he has created, and he can restore us to wholeness even when we fall from grace. Remember that Bathsheba and David later had a son named Solomon, who became the wisest man of all time. Even in the midst of sin and dysfunction, God receives glory when we confess our sins and return to his path.

—M. Williams

Reflect on a time in your life when God received glory in the midst of your sin and dysfunction. Thank God for his grace.

Read: 2 Samuel 11:1—12:25; 1 Kings 1:11–31; 2:13–25.

TAMAR
A Violated Woman

Tamar is a role model for any woman who has ever tried to do right but was treated wrongly. From the account of Amnon and Tamar, it appears that Tamar was a respectable young woman who wanted to play by the rules. When her father, King David, instructed her to make a meal for her half-brother Amnon, Tamar did just as she was told (see 2Sa 13:7–8). When her unscrupulous brother told her to serve him alone in his bedroom, Tamar did as she was instructed (see vv. 8–10). Even as Amnon grabbed her, Tamar pleaded with him to stop and follow the rules (see vv. 12–14). She told him that if he would just ask the king for her hand in marriage, they could be married and have sex "the right way." While Amnon thought he was in love with her, we see that Amnon used her to gratify his immediate desires and then despised her.

Many of us are in situations like Tamar's. We've tried to live according to God's Word, we've obeyed the laws of the land, but somehow we still keep getting violated. Someone betrays our trust, someone manipulates our generosity, and before we know it, we're left living with the consequences of other people's poor choices and sinful acts.

Tamar

Second Samuel 13:20 describes what happened to Tamar after the rape. She could not marry, so she lived with her brother Absalom as a desolate, broken and violated woman. What can we learn from this tragic story?

While it's hard to find anything positive here, it does force us to rethink how we treat victims. Do we cast aside those who struggle in life and live desolate, broken lives? Or do we remind them of the healing power of Christ? Do we share the stories of how Jesus took the time to speak to those who were the castaways of society? Do we show the same love Christ showed to the downtrodden? With the love of Christ, we who try to do right and end up getting wronged do not have to live defeated lives. Our brokenness can be restored and our tragedies can become testimonies of the true, unconditional love of Christ. Let Tamar's story remind us to extend a hand and the love of Jesus to those who have been violated in any way.

—K. Washington

How do you treat your sisters who are struggling? What can you do today to help someone who has been victimized?

Read: 2 Samuel 13.

Rizpah

A Grieving Mother

Rizpah is a relatively unknown woman of the Scriptures, yet her actions speaker louder than words.

In Rizpah we see a mother who demonstrated love and compassion in order to preserve the remains of not only her two sons, but also her stepdaughter's five sons.

She took sackcloth—a symbol of mourning and distress—and placed it on a rock for herself. The men had been put to death at the beginning of the barley harvest in April (see 2Sa 21:9). Rizpah kept watch over the bodies to protect them from the vultures and jackals "till the rain poured down from the heavens" (2Sa 21:10). Though this may have been a special God-sent rain, marking the end of God's judgment via drought, alternatively this reference could have been to the normal rainy season in October. Seven men were executed for their father's/grandfather's sin; for as long as six months, Rizpah dealt with their deaths, face to face.

When King David heard of Rizpah's vigil, he was moved by her example and provided a proper burial both for these seven men and for Saul and Jonathan. While Rizpah couldn't save her sons' lives, her courageous protection of their bodies after death was rewarded (see 2Sa 21:11–14). Rizpah prompted an act that blessed the entire land.

Mothers all over this nation, especially African American mothers, have found themselves in Rizpah's position. They find themselves taking on the vultures by day and the jackals by night. Today's vultures and jackals include racism and the drug culture that destroys everything that gets in its way. The phenomenon of crack strikes at the central nervous system of our community. It can make African American children turn on their own mothers and African American women give up their children—something even slavery couldn't do.

Statistics continue to knock at the door with tragic news. Each day many of our mothers learn that their children have been harmed in some way—socially, economically, educationally, psychologically, spiritually or physically. We must grieve; we must pick up our sackcloth and grieve over the situations that now confront us. We must keep vigil over the injustice done to our children. Even if and when some die, we must keep pressing for justice and honor. Through the prayers of mothers, through the vigils of mothers and through the fight of mothers, others can be saved, and our land can be healed.

—R. Walker

For what or for whom do you feel compelled to keep a vigil until justice is done? Pray and fight for justice.

Read: 2 Samuel 3:6–11; 21:1–14.

The Queen of Sheba

In Search of True Wisdom

The queen of Sheba, also known as the Queen of the South (see Mt 12:42; Lk 11:31), was perhaps one of the most powerful women of her day.

Scholars generally agree that she reigned over territory in southwest Arabia (modern Yemen) and across the Red Sea from northeast Africa. The name Sheba (or Seba) implies that this queen was a woman of color. Sheba is mentioned as a grandson of Keturah, Abraham's second wife (see Ge 25:1–4; 1Ch 1:32; see the African Presence Notes on Genesis 25:1–2 and Exodus 2:16–22).

As we look at the exchange of gifts between the queen of Sheba and Solomon (see 1Ki 10:10–13; 2Ch 9:9–12), several points deserve further consideration. First, she came bearing gifts. The area from which the queen of Sheba came was known for both gold and spices. She gave the king 120 talents (about 4.5 tons) of gold and scores of spices and jewels. Jewish historians give her credit for introducing the cultivation of certain spices, like balsam, to Israel. The kinds of gifts she gave and the quantities of those gifts had never been seen in Israel.

Second, notice the gifts that Solomon gave the queen of Sheba. Though Solomon was known for being generous with his many guests, he was reported to have been exceptionally generous with the queen of Sheba. He gave her anything her heart desired. The total of the gifts he gave her exceeded what she had given him (see 2Ch 9:12). They appear to have made a profound impression upon one another. His wisdom and opulence awed the queen. And even though she was a woman of enormous wealth and wisdom, Solomon's magnificent wealth and wisdom overwhelmed her. And out of respect for him, she gave the highest praise to his God. God later gave the queen of Sheba a great tribute also: He used her to show the Pharisees how foolish they were (see Mt 12:42).

Solomon, who was reported to have had 700 wives and 300 concubines, obviously had special regard for this powerful woman of color who sought out wisdom for herself. Jewish tradition tells us that Solomon and the queen of Sheba parented a son, believed to be King Menelek.

—S. Fosua

What price are you willing to pay to gain true wisdom? Are you willing to give up some things to seek God fully?

Read: 1 Kings 10:1–13; 2 Chronicles 9:1–12; Matthew 12:42.

THE PROPHET'S WIDOW

God Provides

The widow was the least of all people in ancient society. Upon her husband's death, his inheritance passed to his sons. If she had no children, she was

returned to her father's household. Thus, her vulnerable state made her easy prey for a creditor or anyone else who wished to take advantage of an already bad situation. Although the Jewish Scriptures clearly called for mercy and justice for widows (see Dt 14:28–29; 24:19–21; Isa 10:1–2), it obviously wasn't always the reality.

Second Kings 4:1–7 records one widow's plight and the miracle of mercy that restored her. This woman's husband had been part of a rather unique and closed community within Israel—that of the prophets. Yet she was no less vulnerable than other widows were. Her back was against the wall, and her creditors were about to take her only means of survival—her two sons. Her story describes a marvelous truth that God works with what we have to do miraculous things! When she appealed to the prophet Elisha, he asked what she had in her house (2Ki 4:2). It was from a simple jar of oil that God met her needs. As she poured out the oil—in obedience to Elisha's instruction—she witnessed God's abundant love. God provided her with the means to pay her creditors and to support her family.

How often do we overlook what is in our "house" that God wants to use? We might look for great things and great people to move on our behalf, and yet these things and these people are powerless without God's intervention.

It is interesting that the widow mentioned oil as the one thing of value or usefulness in her house. Oil is a symbol of the indwelling presence of the Holy Spirit. In the parable of the ten virgins, recorded in Matthew 25, we are reminded to keep the lamp of our hearts filled with oil—the Holy Spirit—to ensure that the bridegroom (Jesus) knows that we are prepared and anxiously awaiting his return. Again, God will use what is in our "house" in that final miracle of mercy.

The prophet's widow exemplifies God's concern for women. Through her example, we see our need to have faith and to obey God's will. God will take care of the rest.

—L. Caldwell

Ask God to show you what you have in your possession that he can use to make good out of a bad situation.

Read: 2 Kings 4:1–7.

The Shunammite Woman

Our Sister's Grief Is Our Grief

How do we share our loss or losses with others? What can this unnamed wealthy woman tell us about faith, humility, hospitality and grace? God had the author of 2 Kings record her story to help us deal with our own losses.

A woman of means, the Shunammite woman showed kindness to the prophet Elisha and his servant Gehazi. She provided a room and provision for the itinerant prophet (see 2Ki 4:10). Her reward for humility, hospitality and grace came in the form of a prophecy; Elisha prophesied that she and her elderly husband would bear a son (see 2Ki 4:15). And that prophecy came true. The woman had a baby boy.

In later years, the child died in her arms—the very arms that had held him when he cried, the very arms that had comforted him when he was ill, the very arms that had fed him when he could not feed himself, and the very arms that had taught him to love the Lord. Yet, although filled with grief, she held on to the fact that the prophet of God had foretold the gift of her son. Could we lay our child down and walk away? Could we hold fast to the promises of God? The Shunammite woman's faith and confident determination in the midst of grief resulted in the restoration of her son's life.

Miracles happen to us daily. Our grievous losses are sometimes precursors to hidden miracles yet to be revealed. Our faith unlocks the key to our understanding. As we journey through this story, we can envision the many blessings that unfolded for this Shunammite wife and mother. And we can anticipate our own miracles in the midst of our grief.

—B. Kitt

What miracles have come out of grievous situations in your life? Share your testimony with someone who needs to hear it.

Read: 2 Kings 4:8–37; 8:1–6.

Jezebel

Call Me Bitter
A Wicked Queen

Evil, idolatrous and an abuser of power are just a few of the descriptions associated with Queen Jezebel. However, even from her story, women of color can learn valuable lessons.

Jezebel grew up in a home and community of idol worshipers. She brought her own religious beliefs with her when she married King Ahab, and her influence contributed to the widespread worship of idols in Israel. Jezebel influenced both the king and the country, and Ahab's reign was characterized as evil in part as a result of his reliance on his wife and her views (see 1Ki 16:31; 21:25–26).

Elijah was one of God's prophets during the reign of Ahab and Jezebel. Elijah challenged the 450 prophets of Baal and 400 prophets of Asherah to call on their god to send fire upon an altar; of course they were unsuccessful. Elijah prayed to God to send fire on an altar that Elijah had first soaked in water. The true and living God produced fire. After Elijah won this amazing challenge, he ordered the deaths of all of the prophets of Baal and Asherah (see 1Ki 18:40; 19:1). When Jezebel heard what Elijah had done to the prophets of the gods she worshiped, she sent a message to Elijah, threatening to kill him by the next day (see 1Ki 19:2).

It has been said that the test of a true prophet is that his or her prediction comes true. Jezebel's prediction about taking Elijah's life did not come true. Elijah ran away and hid from Jezebel's wrath, but Yahweh protected, fed and sheltered him (see 1Ki 19:3–9). Conversely, Elijah prophesied about Jezebel's destruction as well as her family's demise (see 1Ki 21:20–24), and she died just as Elijah prophesied: dogs devoured her so that no one could recognize her body (see 2Ki 9:30–37). Ahab and Jezebel's evil choices contributed to their own deaths, the deaths of the prophets of Baal and the deaths of the 70 sons of Ahab (see 1Ki 22:34–38; 2Ki 10:7).

Sometimes it seems like the wicked prosper and the righteous suffer, but this story reminds us that there is a day of judgment coming. Regardless of how things seem, eventually the righteous will receive shelter, as was true with Elijah, and evil will have its own reward, as was seen through the deaths of Ahab, Jezebel and their children.

—D. McCabe

Reflect on times when it looked like the wicked were prospering. How did things turn out? Seek to live life on God's side regardless of how things look around you.

Read: 1 Kings 16:29–33; 18:16—19:9; 21:4–26; 2 Kings 9:10,22,30–37. 9:10,22,30–37.

Huldah
A Prophetess of God

One of the great stories of a woman prophet in the Bible is found in 2 Kings 22. The prophet's name was Huldah. Not much is recorded of her life, but the story of one event in her life serves to create an unforgettable profile of a woman called by God.

Huldah lived in Jerusalem during the reign of Josiah. This king of Judah, unlike his father and grandfather, "did what was right in the eyes of the Lord" (2Ki 22:2). Hilkiah, the high priest, discovered the Book of the Law in the temple. When King Josiah heard the neglected words of Scripture, he responded with grief and repentance. Josiah then sent members of his cabinet to inquire of the Lord's pending judgment on his people. They sought counsel from the prophetess Huldah. God used Huldah to deliver messages to the king (see 2Ki 22:14–20). It is noteworthy that Huldah was consulted rather than Jeremiah, the well-known prophet who also ministered at this time (compare 2Ki 22:3 and Jer

1:2). This demonstrates that God doesn't assign women secondary status, nor does he use women for ministry only when there are no men available.

Huldah's brief biography mentions only that she was married to a man named Shallum and that she lived in the Second District of Jerusalem (see 2Ki 22:14; see also 2Ch 34:22). That's all! Yet the king's men sought her for counsel. The common cord that linked Huldah with the leader of the country and members of the king's cabinet was that they wanted to do what was pleasing in God's sight.

While little else is known about Huldah, we know the most important thing about her: She desired to do God's will. When people think of you, will they remember you as a Huldah? Will they say you wanted to follow God?

—M. Armstead

Reflect on a time when others sought you out for counsel. Did you share God's Word with them or did you tell them what they wanted to hear?

Read: 2 Kings 22:1–20; 2 Chronicles 34:14–28.

JEHOSHEBA
Standing Firm

Jehosheba was the daughter of King Jehoram, king of Judah, and the savior of the heir to the throne. Jehoram had married Athaliah, a daughter of Ahab (Israel's evil, idolatrous king). After the deaths of Jehoram and his successor, Athaliah's son Ahaziah, Athaliah's lust for power led her to kill off all those of the house of David who were the rightful heirs to the throne. Never mind that these heirs happened to be her own grandsons! Athaliah became one of the most detestable rulers of Judah and the only queen of Judah to rule in her own name.

Jehosheba was likely Athaliah's stepdaughter, the daughter of Jehoram by another wife. She was used by God to rescue her infant nephew Joash. She hid him and his nurse in a bedroom right before the other royal princes were murdered (see 2Ch 22:11). And she continued to keep him hidden for six years in the temple of the Lord (see 2Ch 22:12). The temple provided a safe place for Joash and an environment in which he could be prepared for his future as king. During that time Queen Athaliah ruled with a vengeance, never knowing that one of the legitimate heirs to the throne was under her nose the entire time. By rescuing Joash, Jehosheba became an instrument of God in his divine plan to keep his promise that a son of David would always be king.

Today there are many who despise the name of Jesus Christ and will behave as Queen Athaliah in an attempt to destroy God's people. But believers must stand firm and trust God to determine the outcome of our enemy's plans. Whatever God's plans are for us, no amount of adversity can thwart them.

As Christian women we are to encourage one another. Whatever trials we face, we can trust our Lord to hide us in the shadow of his wings and cause our enemies to become our footstools.

—J. Josey

Reflect on the fact that God's plans will not be thwarted. Rejoice in the plan God has for your life.

Read: 2 Kings 11:1–3; 2 Chronicles 22:10–12.

Athaliah
An Angry Woman

Athaliah, at a glance, appears to be nothing short of wicked; she's hard-core, low-down, good for nothing and rotten to the bone. How often, after all, do you hear of a woman murdering her own grandchildren to grasp power—like she did following the deaths of her husband and son, the kings of Judah (see 2Ch 22:10–11)? Growing up in the royal family of the northern kingdom of Israel, Athaliah was the granddaughter of the idolatrous King Omri and the daughter of none other than the notorious King Ahab, who was married to Jezebel. (Though it is uncertain, some believe that Jezebel was Athaliah's mother.) Talk about a generational curse! The makeup of Athaliah's life is nothing short of a counselor's nightmare.

Imagine coming from the family into which she was born. Though her family had power and money, they are remembered for their evil choices and idolatry. Athaliah grew up in a palace steeped in Baal worship. Such a life certainly influenced her later choices. She became a woman who was power-hungry, violent and evil.

Prisons, detention centers and rehabs are full of Athaliahs—angry women who lash out violently at anybody and everybody, trusting no one. Athaliahs believe that anger and violence are the realities of life. After all, that's the way it was with her mama and her mama before her.

Athaliahs tend to deny that their own anger is the problem. They usually blame their problems on something else: "I'm black. I'm poor. I'm fat. I'm ugly. Everybody's always picking on me." Athaliahs tend to see themselves as victims. This thinking ultimately produces what the very thing it believes. But the excuse of victimization becomes a prison, trapping them in their own anger. Letting go of their anger at the world is often difficult to do, but letting go is the only way for them to give their burdens to Jesus and let him truly love them. Athaliahs have to evaluate the past, release unhealthy patterns and learn new patterns to live healthy and whole lives as daughters of God.

—E. Walters

What unhealthy patterns from your past do you need to release? Remember that you are God's beautiful daughter—regardless of what kind of earthly family you come from.

Read: 2 Kings 8:25–27; 2 Chronicles 21:4—23:21.

QUEEN VASHTI
A Woman of Strength

King Xerxes, the ruler of 127 provinces from India to Cush (the upper Nile region, south of Egypt), gave a banquet for all his underlings—probably in an attempt to rally support for an invasion of Greece. He and his royal cabinet and provincial leaders partied for 180 days—six months. This probably meant six months of drinking, telling tall tales and more drinking—plus whatever unmentionable things they could think of doing. An after-party, which also included all the local residents, lasted another seven days.

While the men became drunk at their party, Queen Vashti gave a party for the women. On the seventh day of the after-party, the king sent seven eunuchs to get Queen Vashti. She was told to come to the men's party wearing the royal crown. She was his trophy, and he wanted to show her off.

Queen Vashti

The eunuchs came to the queen to deliver King Xerxes' message, but she would not come (see Est 1:12). She would not be made to look like a fool to these provincial women to whom she was an example of all that a woman could be. Now, she was not ignorant of the price she would have to pay, but she was willing to challenge the king's drunken foolishness in order to be true to herself. This woman was a strong sister—willing to take a chance for the good that she might be able to do for those who came behind her.

Sometimes we have to step out there and be an example so that those who follow will know what can be done. Strength and wisdom are qualities that each of us needs to rely on God for and encourage in our sisters.

We have but to remember our history: Hatshepsut, the Egyptian queen of the Eighteenth Dynasty; the beautiful warrior queen Makeda; Ann Zingha, the amazon queen of Matamba, West Africa; Sojourner Truth; Harriet Tubman; Mary McLeod Bethune; Marian Anderson; Barbara Jordan; Fannie Lou Hamer; and Rosa Parks, as well as the women you have been blessed to observe.

—M. Bellinger

Reflect on the strength and wisdom of women you know. Ask God for strength and wisdom to guide you through this day.

Read: Esther 1.

ESTHER
More Than a Beauty Queen

The story of Esther reminds women of color that our outward beauty is not the only, or the most important, characteristic we have been blessed to receive. Esther spent 12 months enhancing her physical appearance (see Est 2:12). And she clearly had it going on. She won the favor of King Xerxes over all of the other young ladies who were being pampered and prepared to be queen. She was definitely beautiful.

However, Esther's true worth didn't come from her beauty, and it is not her beauty that has left a lasting impression on Bible readers throughout history. This beauty queen had to make a decision once she heard from her cousin Mordecai about a plan to destroy the Jewish people who lived throughout the empire. She had to approach the king and ask him to stop this plan, to revoke the edict he had been convinced to decree, and to spare her people's lives. She had to be brave to approach the king, so she called for the people to fast; and we remember her famous words: "And if I perish, I perish" (Est 4:16). Esther remembered her people, and she was willing to sacrifice her life to save them.

Esther shows us that we are called to help others, regardless of our position. When we have influence in high places, we should use that influence to help those less fortunate than ourselves. We should use that influence to fight for justice rather than to merely gain a position that makes us look good. Esther reminds us that it's not all about how we look; it's about what we do. While we pour time and money into making sure we look good, let's make sure we do good—even when we have to take risks.

—K. Washington

How have you used your influence to help others or help determine the outcome of a situation? Pray for the courage of Esther to do the right thing no matter what the circumstances.

Read: Esther 2–8.

Job's Wife

She Was Tested Too

There was once a woman who lived in the land of Uz. She had a husband by the name of Job. The Bible says that he was a faithful man. Can we not assume that she was a faithful woman also?

They had seven sons and three daughters. They had numerous livestock and a number of servants. Job is described as "the greatest man among all the people of the East" (Job 1:3), so we can assume that Job's wife was the greatest woman.

Then, at the hand of Satan, the test came. It is traditionally called "Job's Test," but it was "Mrs. Job's Test" as well. Their livestock and servants were destroyed, their assets were lost and all ten of their children were killed.

The Biblical camera then focuses on Job's grief, giving no attention to Mrs. Job. Indeed, the heavenly wager that had been placed on her husband had destroyed her world too. The pain intensified when her husband was stricken with sores all over his body. We should not be surprised that her faith faltered and she cried out to Job, "Are you still holding on to your integrity? Curse God and die!" (Job 2:9). These are the words that have provoked commentators, past and present, to scorn Mrs. Job. Although Satan surely used her words to tempt Job (compare Job 2:9 with Job 2:5), anyone who has experienced great loss can understand her outburst.

She, too, suffered as she watched the one she loved endure such great pain. She also was in mourning, for she also had lost her sons and daughters. It is probable that she suggested death to Job because death is what she wished for herself. She felt that faith and courage were unattainable at that moment. Furthermore, haven't we all said things for which we have had to repent?

Job's Wife

Job 42:10–13 tells us that the Lord blessed the latter part of Job's life with double the earthly possessions and ten more children. We can safely assume that the mother of the last ten children was the mother of the first ten. Restoration and reconciliation, then, were Mrs. Job's, just as they were Job's. As we reflect on this beleaguered woman, we can find comfort in the hope of restoration and reconciliation when we endure suffering.

—M. Flake

Do you need restoration and reconciliation? Reflect on the story of Job's wife to inspire you to keep your faith in God. Share her story with someone you know who needs restoration and reconciliation.

Read: Job 1:1—2:10; 42:10–13.

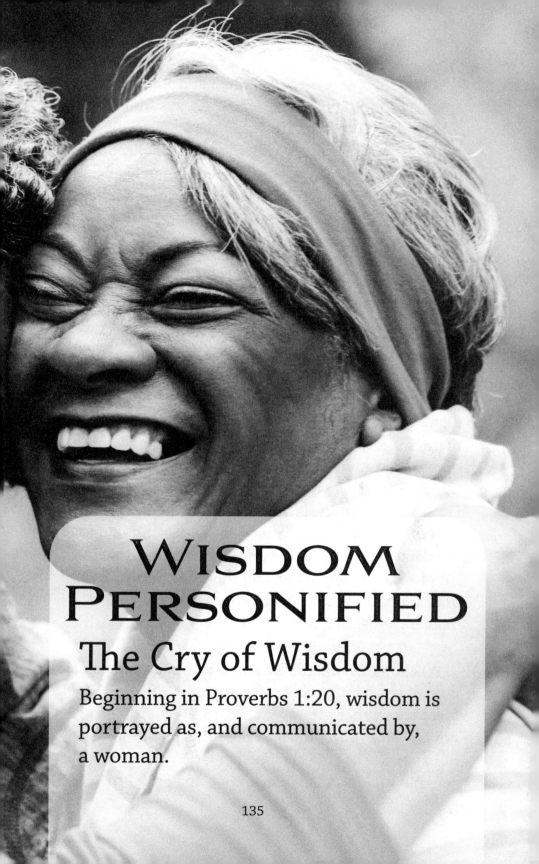

WISDOM PERSONIFIED
The Cry of Wisdom

Beginning in Proverbs 1:20, wisdom is portrayed as, and communicated by, a woman.

This reveals that there has been, and still can be, an image of femininity that personifies wisdom. This concept in the book of Proverbs calls us to establish the expectation that women will bring to the solution of the world's problems a precious perspective not available from any other source. It calls us to provide a fresh stimulus of challenge and a freeing of dormant powers because wisdom can be and is personified in the women of the world.

Wisdom is not portrayed as the cold, objective, dispassionate scholar. Instead, she cries her message all over town. She has a strange conviction that she cannot repress, and her "scholarship" is so centered on human concerns that she exceeds the bounds of dignity. Because she is in dialogue with people at the market, the courts, the highways and the lofty walls of mass communication, she will not be caught out of touch with human realities and existential concerns. Perhaps because she is a mother as well as a sage, she cannot view that which affects mothers' children with the detachment of a professor. She demands that her insights be implemented, and she is the personification of passionate practicality, as opposed to the almost helpless female.

Wisdom demands application. She insists on being a doer of truth rather than a hearer only. The fact that she must cry out her message seems to suggest that she does not have the power to apply her principles arbitrarily. But she does not hide behind her lack of authority. She goes out and risks her image, choosing rather to have tried and lost than never to have tried at all. Wisdom is not a distant dilettante or pretty patron. She rolls up her sleeves and goes to work. She goes out into the marketplace.

Wisdom must never cease her cry. And we must never cease to expect her to cry out and save us. If we do, we will perish.

—E. Mitchell

How will you apply wisdom? Live as a wise woman today.

Read: Proverbs 1:20–33.

THE ADULTERESS OF PROVERBS

The Path to Death

Proverbs 5–7 gives a loud warning about involvement with the adulteress.

The adulteress is an immoral woman and an unfaithful wife. She heads down a crooked path that leads to death. Her seductive speech is deceptive and cunning, resulting in an unhealthy, heart-crushing experience.

Her marriage vows are openly broken and disregarded. She has forgotten the covenant words of God. She describes the sex act to lure the man to her bed (see Prov 7:16–18). Her trap is set during the night; she approaches boldly, dressed like a prostitute (vv. 10–19), inviting the man to her house, assuring him of their privacy (vv. 19–20), and while flattering him, she then traps him (see Prov 7:21–23).

The adulteress wants to possess the soul of her victim and take his strength. She causes a wound and brings dishonor to his life (Prov 6:33). His life is stricken in many ways: his body may become diseased (Prov 5:11); he may become publicly disgraced (Prov 5:14); and his soul may be destroyed (Prov 6:32; 7:27).

Proverbs gives several ways a man can avoid the adulteress: He must pay attention to wisdom (Prov 5:1), avoid the adulteress's door (Prov 5:8), keep the law of God in his heart (Prov 7:1–3), and be ravished always with the sexual love of his wife (Prov 5:15–19).

The African American woman is seen, at times, as the spiritual strength of the family. When the adulteress taints her life, it is devastating to her marriage and spirit. It poisons the husband-wife relationship, breaking trust, and it eats away at the wife's ability to love. She can lose the ability to fulfill the marriage commitment, be afraid to trust, and avoid openness with her spouse. Sad to say, adultery can lead to divorce, which divides her family and makes trusting another man difficult.

The adulteress is no one to envy, for her path leads to destruction. But Jesus can forgive her sins (see Jn 8:1–11) and create a clean heart within her. She can become a woman devoted to Jesus, and she can receive eternal life, instead of being a woman who leads another life to death. Certainly the Word of God provides a healing balm and guiding light for every woman.

—G. London

How has the Word of God provided a healing balm and guiding light for you? Share your testimony with a woman who needs to hear some good news today.

Read: Proverbs 5–7.

A Virtuous Woman

A Strong Woman, Dependent on God

While the NIV refers to the woman of Proverbs 31 as a "wife of noble character" (Pr 31:10), many of us have grown up calling her the "virtuous woman" (KJV).

The virtuous woman in Proverbs 31 selects wool and flax, works with willing hands, brings her household food, gets up while it is still dark, buys fields, plants vineyards and so on. The word virtuous implies strength, and this proverb extols the dignity of women and emphasizes the importance of motherhood and home. A virtuous woman has strength and honor, and she is able to bear up under many crosses and disappointments.

How many of us have held up under corporate America's glass ceiling, sexism in the workplace, racism, unruly children, divorce and single parenthood? A virtuous woman speaks words that are wise and kind. She knows how to temper her words and hold her peace if need be. She takes care of her household, meaning she can make a meal out of nothing or stretch a week's worth of food into four weeks' worth; she can cook and clean with a baby on her hip while helping another child with homework. All of us can see ourselves in this virtuous woman.

But how do we maintain our virtue? How are we able to remain strong? It is through our reverence of God and submission to his will. We must put God above everything in our lives. We must seek him; we must serve him; we must witness to others about him; we must love him with all our hearts, with all our souls and with all our minds. Proverbs 31:30–31 says, "Charm is deceptive, and beauty is fleeting; but a woman who fears the Lord is to be praised. Give her the reward she has earned, and let her works bring her praise at the city gate." We strong women earn our reward by knowing

God and seeking to please him and by depending on God for wisdom to care for ourselves and our families.

The Scriptures don't tell us who the woman in Proverbs 31 was—only what she was. A closer look at the virtuous woman can provide invaluable assistance to women today who are trying desperately to balance their lives and walk in God's will.

—T. Booker

How often do you seek God first before you begin the many tasks you have to do? Begin each task today with a talk with God. Seek God's guidance and wisdom throughout the day.

Read: Proverbs 31:10–31.

The Bridegroom & His Bride

Soul Mates in Life

The Shulammite bride in Song of Songs has been described as many different things. She has been classified as rich, poor, a commoner and a princess. But she was first and foremost a woman in love.

She was a woman who endured much to be with the one she loved. The bride spoke of their courtship, remembering how the groom looked and behaved toward her.

The bride spoke of her engagement to her man, of misunderstandings, and of her restless thoughts when separated from him. The length of their separation and her longing for him troubled her sleep—not once, but twice. She longed for her best friend, her banner, her lover and her lord. Even as she went about her daily tasks, her mind was on the love of her life, the man who had swept her off her feet with kind words, gentle strength and tender embraces.

When the bride and bridegroom finally were reunited, it was with a joy reserved for people who have endured misunderstandings, temptations and pain in order to be together. Alternately passionate and shy, the bride built up her husband, loving him with the sweetness of her words and body. While she was jealous of him, she still loved him with all of her being. Her husband was her friend—implying that they were soul mates before they consummated their union.

The relationship between the bride and her husband personifies love in its purest form—a monogamous relationship between a husband and wife who have an abiding respect and a replete and unassuming trust. This same desire is found in the spiritual relationship of knowing Jesus as Lord. We are to love him with the same passion and all-consuming fire, the same jealousy, abiding love and respect with which we would love our spouse. We must come to Jesus, our Bridegroom, with the same unabashed love that he demonstrates daily to Christians, those whom he considers his bride.

—M. Cotton Bohanon

Do you long for Jesus as much as the bride longed for her lover? Fall in love with the Lord all over again today. Think about all he has done for you and all he means to you throughout the day.

Read: Song of Songs.

Ezekiel's Wife

On God's Stage

Ezekiel and his wife were among a group of Israelites who had been exiled to Babylon. Once there, the Lord called Ezekiel, a priest, to prophesy to his fellow exiles. Ezekiel was forewarned of his wife's death, but he was compelled by God not to mourn or do the normal ceremonial things associated with grieving (see Eze 24:15–17). The death of his wife was to be a sign to the people of the impending fall of Jerusalem.

Ezekiel's wife is unnamed, but we may assume that she was a godly woman. God called her the "delight" of Ezekiel's eyes (Eze 24:16). It is obvious that to Ezekiel, she was beloved. Ezekiel is one of the most dramatic prophets in the Scriptures. His ministry was one of acting out the word of the Lord to the people. It appears that Ezekiel's wife was accustomed to having her life portrayed as if on stage. Furthermore, since Ezekiel occasionally met with the elders of the people in his house (see Eze 8:1; 14:1; 20:1), we can assume that his wife was a hospitable hostess. Because of the dramatic demonstrations Ezekiel enacted before the people to communicate God's message, his wife surely must have had a keen sense of God herself. From one

Ezekiel's Wife

moment to the next, Ezekiel was caught up in unusual behavior. Much of his book is prophetic, poetic and symbolic; therefore, we might assume that Ezekiel's wife experienced firsthand the actions and poetry of love.

Ezekiel was told that his grief following his wife's sudden death was to be experienced in silence. This was because God wanted to demonstrate to Israel that what they had loved would be destroyed, and, because of theirs sins, they would waste away in remorse rather than mourn in a healthy way (see Eze 24:23). Ezekiel and his wife were used by God to demonstrate the heartbreak of disobedience.

We often do not know what role we are playing on this stage of life. God has a purpose for all that is done in our lives. Yet because we are often not the main character, we feel obscure. The story of Ezekiel's wife speaks to those of us who maintain our place of love but never see its impact during our lifetime. She died to promote God's truth that we must love the Lord and obey the Lord no matter what the circumstances.

—D. Shumake JaPhia

Determine to play your role in life faithfully and well. You never know how God is using you to touch someone else. Reflect on one thing you will do faithfully and well today.

Read: Ezekiel 24.

Gomer
An Unfaithful Wife

On the surface the story of Gomer is filled with pain and disappointment, yet her story does shed light on God's forgiveness. Gomer is used to show us how much God loves us, cares for us and is willing to forgive us.

Gomer was the wife of the prophet Hosea. God instructed Hosea to marry Gomer, an adulterous woman (see Hos 1:2). Gomer's behavior is used throughout the prophetic book of Hosea as symbolic of Israel. Just as Gomer was an unfaithful wife, Israel had been unfaithful to God.

Hosea and Gomer had children, and their babies were named according to God's directives. They, too, were used to show what God would do to his unfaithful people: Jezreel means "God scatters" and refers to punishment; Lo-Ruhamah means "not loved"; and Lo-Ammi means "not my people."

Although Gomer was guilty of being unfaithful during her marriage, God instructed Hosea to reconcile with his wife. Hosea was told to show love to his wife, just as the Lord loved the Israelites even though they were unfaithful. So Hosea obediently purchased his unfaithful wife from slavery (see Hos 3:1–3).

While the story of Israel was a cycle of obedience and disobedience, and it was filled with the blessings and curses of God, we can't help but read the prophets and think of God's grace and love. It is clear that God loved Israel and loves us. However, we, just as the Israelites did, break God's heart time and time again. While we often have to live with the consequences of our bad decisions, we can find joy and hope in reconciliation with God, who is ready and willing to receive us when we repent. God wants to be in relationship with us. God wants to love us—it's evident in the gift of Christ.

Yes, unfaithful ones, we have a chance to be reconciled to our faithful God, our true lover.

—K. Washington

Have you repented for your unfaithfulness? God is ready and willing to be reconciled with you. Share this good news with another sister today!

Read: Hosea 1–3.

New Testament

THE CANAANITE WOMAN
Persistence Pays Off

When the worst of our troubles attack us, as wise women we know whom to go to get help. Our sister, the Canaanite woman, knew where to go and whom to see. She knew what Jesus could do. Can you image what she was like? A small woman, nothing notable, just hot and tired, lines of worry deeply etched in her face. She got to Jesus, and the disciples had the nerve to try to send her away because she was bothering them! The disciples didn't recognize that this woman was on a mission. To her, it didn't matter if Jesus was trying to rest or if the disciples didn't want her there. She had made up her mind. She wasn't leaving.

When the Canaanite woman faced Jesus (see both Mt 15:21–28 and Mk 7:24–30), Jesus responded to her request in a seemingly negative manner. He questioned her and tested her faith. But Jesus' seemingly harsh words did not deter the woman from her goal. When we are worried and scared for our children, we don't tolerate obstacles put in our way. This woman persisted. She was determined and pressed her case with Jesus. In effect, she said to him, "I know that God sent you first to the Jews, not to us Gentiles. But look at me. You are my last hope, and you know it. Can you really turn me away? Can you really let my child continue to suffer?" Sisters, have you been there?

The Canaanite woman persisted. Jesus heard her. He was impressed with her persistence and faith. Her faith was so great that she was able to withstand any obstacles. She placed her trust soundly in Christ. Like her, we cannot give up, turn around or turn away. Like her, we must have strong faith in Jesus.

—M. Bellinger

Do you feel like giving up? Persist! Don't be discouraged, no matter what others say. Continue to seek God and take your burdens to him.

Read: Matthew 15:21–28; Mark 7:24–30.

Wise and Foolish Virgins
Preparing for Christ

Many who read the parable of the ten virgins in Matthew 25 wonder how it can fit with the notion of Jesus Christ as the compassionate, merciful Savior. After all, was it not Jesus himself who, when asked by Peter how many times he had to forgive those who wronged him, gave the answer of 77 times? Didn't Paul plead with us to be kind, compassionate and forgiving of each other? Isn't one of the most tender and moving passages in the New Testament the one in which Paul requested Philemon to take Onesimus back and not punish him? Think of the parables about the Good Samaritan, who took care of an enemy, and the servant who was punished because he showed no mercy when he himself had received mercy. The Bible is so full of examples of mercy that it seems that the five foolish virgins got a raw deal.

The five foolish virgins, like the five wise virgins, knew exactly what they needed to do. The precise time of the anticipated wedding procession wasn't announced, but the customs of the day told them how to be prepared:

"Bring your lamps. Bring the oil. Trim the wicks. See that you're ready." For whatever reason, the foolish virgins chose not to do so. The five wise virgins, on the other hand, were obedient to do what was required—and therefore they were prepared when the time arrived.

This teaches us several things. First, perhaps we should not question instructions, suggestions and directions we are given—even if they seem mundane, trivial, boring or "beneath" our creativity, uniqueness and specialness. Sometimes we just don't know the full picture and should trust instructions given by God.

Second, obedience is better than sacrifice. How badly will it hurt us to follow the instructions? We should remember to compare the consequences of obedience and disobedience before we act.

This parable tells us to be ready because we don't know when Christ will call us. Just because he didn't come today doesn't mean he's not coming tonight or tomorrow. Therefore, we must be obedient, consistent and committed to the glory and honor of God. We cannot be found unprepared like the five foolish virgins.

—A. Bouie

How good are you at listening to instructions from God? From others? Pray for wisdom to weigh the cost of obedience and disobedience before acting.

Read: Matthew 24:42—25:13; 1 Thessalonians 5:1–6.

Mary Magdalene
Setting Her Reputation Straight

Mary Magdalene is specifically mentioned 14 times in the Gospels. On nine occasions she is in the company of other women, and the fact that she is usually named first suggests that she more than likely played a leadership role among Jesus' female followers.

All four Gospels note that Mary was among the witnesses of Christ's resurrection. And depending on which Gospel you are reading, either Jesus or an angel commissioned her to go and tell the disciples that he had risen from the dead. This commissioning to "go and tell" is an affirmation for contemporary women; Jesus was and is intentionally gender-inclusive, establishing the place of women in the proclamation of the gospel through Mary.

But who was this woman before her encounters with Christ? Some have said she was a prostitute. If Mary was indeed a prostitute, to have omitted this important fact from her title is contrary to the way in which Biblical writers typically reported the stories in the Scriptures. A case in point is Rahab, an Old Testament woman (see Jos 2:1–22; 6:22–25) who is listed in the New Testament among the faithful servants, yet she never escaped the stigma of the title "prostitute" (Heb 11:31; Jas 2:25).

More important than the fact that Mary Magdalene is presumed to have been a prostitute is the condition from which Jesus liberated her: She had been possessed with seven demons, a fact mentioned in both Mark 16:9 and Luke 8:2. Old Testament scholar Renita Weems, in Just a Sister Away (San Diego: LuraMedia, 1988), ventures to name those seven demons—using names that collectively describe mental, emotional and spiritual conditions that women of all ages have struggled with. They are depression, fear, low self-esteem, doubt, procrastination, bitterness and self-pity. We could add to this list: jealousy, guilt, envy, discord, idolatry and an unforgiving spirit.

But the Great Physician touched Mary Magdalene and made her whole. She became a leader among women, a proclaimer of the gospel to the apostles, an evangelist to the marginalized and a servant in God's kingdom.

For all women, Mary Magdalene is a model of a wounded person who was healed and made whole by the love of Christ, and called and commissioned by him to serve in his kingdom.

—K. Johnson

What issues do you struggle with? Take them to Jesus; ask for God's guidance and wisdom to bring about your healing.

Read: Matthew 28:1–10; Mark 15:40—16:11; Luke 8:1–3; 24:1–11; John 20:1–18.

DAUGHTER OF JAIRUS

A Testament of Faith

A Christian mother, father, grandmother, grandfather, guardian or relative will spend a child's lifetime—from infancy to adulthood—embracing the phrase "Just believe."

These adults, concerned for their beloved children's lives, often find themselves going in prayer to Jesus, the miraculous Master Healer. These adults know that drugs, peer pressure, alcohol, gangs, suicide, depression, low self-esteem, violence, etc. have killed off the innocent or sickened the sons and daughters given to them by God. These believers know that if anyone can rescue their precious children from the deadly ills of society, Jesus certainly can.

We learn in Mark 5:21–24,35–43 that Jairus's pleading for his daughter to Jesus made a difference. Jairus loved his daughter and lifted her name up to Jesus. This caring and loving father continued to believe and have patience when Jesus stopped on the way to Jairus's house. During this stop, Jairus's servants arrived and told him that his daughter was dead. As soon as Jesus heard these words, he gave Jairus the encouragement he needed: "Don't be afraid; just believe" (Mk 5:36).

When Jesus arrived at Jairus's house, people were weeping because the girl was dead. Jesus instructed them to stop weeping, for she was only sleeping (see Mk 5:39). After he removed the doubters and unbelievers from the room, he took the little girl's hand and said, "'Talitha koum!' (which means, 'Little girl, I say to you, get up!')" (Mk 5:41). Immediately, she rose from the grips of death.

Daughter of Jairus

I am certain every adult child who has experienced drugs, alcohol, suicidal thoughts or other deadly temptations can thank God for their parents' desperate prayers to a heavenly Healer and Redeemer who called them to rise above the things that wanted to destroy them. Now they, too, can thank God for Jesus. So parents, pray and plead, plead and pray, and believe that your child—and those around you—will "get up" as Jairus's daughter did.

—D. James

What do you need to "just believe" Jesus for? Seek his guidance and act in faith.

Read: Matthew 9:18–26; Mark 5:21–43; Luke 8:41–56.

HERODIAS & SALOME

Evil Choices

Herodias was a woman out of control. She was politically astute, ambitious, cunning, greedy and would stop at nothing to get what she wanted.

Initially married to Herod Philip, the ruler over the Traconitis and Iturea territories, she eventually left him and married his brother Herod Antipas, who was the ruler over Galilee and Perea and was more powerful than Phillip. John the Baptist spoke against this marriage (see Mk 6:18), and it infuriated her. Herodias became angry to the point of wanting to kill John. King Herod was in awe of John and realized that the people revered him, so he was afraid to have John killed.

King Herod had a birthday celebration during which the daughter of Herodias (we know from the Jewish historian Josephus that her name was Salome) danced—quite sensuously, no doubt—for him and his guests. He became so intoxicated with her dancing that he agreed to give her anything she asked for, up to half his kingdom (see Mk 6:22–23). Herodias saw this as an opportunity to get what she wanted—a chance to have John the Baptist killed. Salome's request caused Herod great sorrow, but he honored his word. As she requested, John's head was delivered on a platter.

The mother-daughter relationship among African Americans can be godly and productive or ungodly and destructive. A daughter's relationship with her mother is the foundation upon which she learns to relate to others. She should be taught to appreciate her beauty, to be honest and to practice godliness in her life. The life of an African American mother may, at times, bring unpleasant and disappointing occurrences. But it is important for a mother to heed the voice of God, which may come through the Scriptures or through other people led by God. Through the Word she can receive correction and direction for every area of life, as well as repentance and forgiveness.

Words are powerful! Words can bring life or death. A mother should speak words of godly instruction into her daughter's life. Words of manipulation, deceit and seduction only bring devastation and death.

—G. London

What relationships with other women in your life have been godly and productive? Which ones have not been so? How can you make your future relationships with sisters godly and productive?

Read: Matthew 14:1–12; Mark 6:14–29; Luke 3:19–20.

The Widow's Offering

Selfless Giving

Jesus sat down in the temple and watched the multitude of people bring their monetary gifts to one of the 13 trumpet-shaped treasury

boxes (see Mk 12:41). Many of the people were wealthy and gave large sums of money. Some gave according to tradition, calculated to the penny by the laws of tithing. One by one they dropped their offerings into the treasury boxes. Quietly, Jesus watched them give funds they did not need for survival.

Jesus noticed a poor widow approach one of the treasury boxes. One could imagine her as an older woman, slightly bent from age. Her head may have been covered with an old cloth, and she probably wore a torn, faded dress. Her fragile, withered hand may have been pressed against her breast, clutching her gift as she walked slowly toward the treasury box. Yet it was not her appearance that drew Jesus' attention. It was her willingness to be obedient to God to the point of giving everything she had. This poor widow dropped two copper coins into the box. These coins were the smallest coins in circulation at that time. But these coins were all she had.

In Jesus' eyes, this woman's gift was greater than all the other gifts combined because her gift constituted all she had. The spirit in which her gift was given made it priceless, for this poor woman had given from her heart. She had given her last in gratitude to God. Jesus was touched by her giving spirit and remarked to his disciples how great her sacrifice was in comparison to the others.

The Widow's Offering

Like the multitude, many of us may give in abundance for self-glorification. Yet Jesus desires that we give of ourselves—our time, talent and money. Jesus calls us to reach beyond the comfortable and give sacrificially. Jesus calls us to be willing to give even our last penny in gratitude to God.

—T. Wade

What is your sacrificial gift to God? Give it joyously to the benefit of God's kingdom.

Read: Mark 12:41–44; Luke 21:1–4.

The Servant Girl

The Truth, the Whole Truth and Nothing but the Truth

Throughout most of his time with Jesus, Simon Peter showed himself strong, brave, loyal and faithful.

He vowed never to deny Jesus, even under the most strenuous circumstances (see Mk 14:29–31). But who was he really? What hidden truth did Jesus know about Peter? Little did Peter know that an unnamed servant girl would reveal a side of him that not even he knew existed.

While warming himself by a fire in the courtyard of the high priest after the arrest of Jesus, Peter was approached by this servant girl. "You also were with that Nazarene, Jesus," she said (Mk 14:67). It was then that Peter first denied any association with Jesus. A second time the girl accused Peter, and again he denied his relationship to Jesus. Jesus was in the process of being interrogated and beaten, and Peter surely feared for his own life. The servant girl and those with her accused Peter again. This time he called down curses on himself if he was lying and swore that he did not know Jesus. In his first two denials, Peter denied being identified with Jesus. In his third denial, he denied Jesus himself.

While Peter had three opportunities to speak the truth, he allowed a spirit of fear and self-preservation to control him. But by lying to the girl and those around her, he was really lying to himself. But he couldn't lie to God. God used both Peter and the servant girl to illustrate to us that even those who profess to love Jesus—even those who follow him and promise to give up their lives for him—can fall into the trap of fear and hopelessness if they do not fully place their trust in him.

Consider how often we lie to others and to ourselves in the midst of unpleasant situations (or keep silent when we know we should speak). How often do we deny God, compromising our trust, loyalty and strength of character in an effort to alleviate the pain or discomfort of a given situation? By God's grace Peter was forgiven (see Lk 24:34; Jn 21:15–19), and the same grace allows us to be forgiven too. Let's remember that when we learn to tell the truth, the whole truth and nothing but the truth—no matter the circumstances—that God is better able to use us for his glory.

—M. Cotton Bohanon

Whom has God used to show you the truth about yourself? Thank God for his grace and mercy. Show grace and mercy to others today.

Read: Mark 14:66–72; see also Matthew 26:69–75; Luke 22:54–62; John 18:15–18, 25–27.

Mary, the Mother of James and Joseph

Sacrificing for Christ

Scripture does not tell us much about the woman whom Matthew twice referred to as "the other Mary" (Mt 27:61; 28:1).

We do know that she was the mother of James (not James the apostle) and Joseph (see Mt 27:56; Mk 15:40). Evidently her sons became well known in the early church.

Mary was likely a woman of some means, as Scripture tells us that she was one of the women who had followed Jesus and "cared for his needs" (Mk 15:41). Mary probably had significant resources, since she was able to leave her home and travel with Jesus, ministering to the physical needs of Jesus and his disciples.

Mary, having followed Jesus during much of his ministry, was a witness to his death on the cross and was among the first to bring spices to the tomb of her Lord (see Mk 15:40; 16:1). Having sacrificed her wealth for the service of Jesus, Mary did not have any regrets and continued to serve him even when all hope looked lost. God honored Mary in a special way: She was among the women who were the first to receive the news that Jesus had risen from the dead (see Mk 16:1–7).

Mary was probably among those in the upper room awaiting the arrival of the promised Holy Spirit on the day of Pentecost, when 3,000 members were added to the church (see Ac 1:4–5,14; 2:1–4,41). At a time when women were not given much consideration or prominence, Mary counted the cost of serving Jesus and determined that, whatever she had to forsake, it was worth the sacrifice.

Mary is an example of a liberated woman, yet she knew that Jesus Christ alone was her liberator. Therefore, she had no need to make demands of anyone for her equality. She knew all too well that God is impartial; he is merciful and full of grace and exalts whom he will. Mary is an excellent example of one who receives the rewards that faith brings. Through her we know that every deed that we do for God counts.

—J. Josey

Reflect on Mary's commitment to Christ. How committed are you to following the way of Christ?

Read: Matthew 27:55—28:10; Mark 15:40—16:8; Luke :1–10.

Mary, the Mother of Jesus
A Model of Motherhood

She is described as "highly favored" (Lk 1:28) and "blessed" (Lk 1:42,45,48). But what makes Mary, the chosen mother of Jesus, worthy of such an honor? What makes Mary a model for motherhood?

Mary was obedient to God's will. Upon hearing the news that she would carry a child, she asked the angel how it was possible for her—a virgin—to have a baby. The angel proceeded to tell Mary that nothing was impossible with God. Mary's response was then: "I am the Lord's servant . . . May it be to me as you have said" (Lk 1:38). Obedient women do not always have to have the plan laid out in black and white for them before they are willing to follow it. Mary trusted God; if this was God's plan, then she was ready to follow it.

Mary was humble. In the Magnificat, her song of praise, Mary rejoiced because God had chosen her to be his servant to deliver Jesus into the world; she did not boast in all she had and why she was the perfect candidate for such an honor. She praised God for choosing her; she didn't list her qualifications but recognized that it was God's grace and mercy that had chosen her for such an honor. The spotlight was not on her; it was placed on the Giver of every good gift—God (see Lk 1:46–55).

Mary was observant. Jesus was not an ordinary child. When Mary and Joseph followed the law of God and presented Jesus in the temple, Simeon and Anna prophesied about the child. Mary and Joseph marveled at their words (see Lk 2:33). Mary no doubt was remembering the promises already made to her about her special child. Scripture also records that, after Jesus stayed behind at the temple as a 12-year-old child, "his mother treasured all these things in her heart" (Lk 2:51).

Mothers of today are smart to pay attention to their children, to observe what they say and what they do. They should also remember that God has plans for their children, and it is their obligation as parents to bring their children up knowing God and the plans he has for his creation.

—K. Washington

How are you like Mary? Pray for a spirit that is humble, observant and obedient to God's will.

Read: Matthew 1:16–25; Luke 1:26—2:52; John 2:1–11; 19:25–27; Acts 1:14.

ANNA
A Model of Spiritual Devotion

Anna was a prophetess. She was a woman through whom God spoke. When she spoke, those in the temple listened. She was a Messianic watcher and a leader. She represents God calling women to be prophetic leaders. She was so respected that her attestation of Jesus was highly regarded, alongside that of an angel and a righteous man (see Lk 2:9–12,25–32,38).

Anna is a model of spiritual devotion. She kept vigil in the temple—fasting, praying and offering thanksgiving. According to Luke 19:45–46, Jesus said that the temple should be a house of prayer, and that is what Anna did there; she prayed.

This devout woman did not allow her circumstances to stop her from worshiping God and waiting for God's promised Messiah. She became a widow after only seven years of marriage, yet she used her situation as an opportunity to devote herself, even until her old age, to interceding for others and setting an example as a worshiper for many to come (see Lk 2:36–37).

Anna was a forerunner to the apostles, who were commissioned to witness to the entire world beginning in Jerusalem (compare Lk 2:38 and Ac 1:8). She joyously told people who the baby Jesus was and what he would do for people. Anna represents hopeful expectation. She is a model who shows women today how to live righteous and godly lives in anticipation of what God will do.

—P. Williams

How can you be more devout in your service to God and others? Use Anna as an example.

Read: Isaiah 9:6–7; Luke 2:36–38.

Peter's Mother-in-Law

From Suffering to Service

The healing of Peter's mother-in-law by Jesus is recorded in all three of the Synoptic Gospels: Matthew, Mark and Luke. Peter's mother-in-law was confined and afflicted with a great fever. The affliction must have been very painful because others sought Jesus on her behalf (see Lk 4:38). Jesus bent over and took her by the hand (see Mk 1:31), and she was healed and immediately rose to minister to them. As a form of gratitude, she served the needs of the Lord and those with him. Her gratitude not only said thank you, but it humbled her for service.

Jesus understood the value of a mother to a family. He also valued women even though society considered them inferior. Each recorded account of Jesus healing a woman speaks to the unique way a woman's life can encounter Jesus. The Scriptures assure African American women of three things:

1. Jesus can touch us and bring healing to any area of our lives on a continuous basis (see Mt 8:14–15; Lk 4:40; 8:53–55). His touch allows us to feel and experience something other than pain.

2. Jesus can lift us up and bring healing to the many painful areas of our lives (see Mk 1:31). We can be elevated emotionally (see Mt 11:28–29), spiritually (see 2Pe 1:3) and physically (see Ro 12:1–2).

3. Jesus can speak to our lives and bring complete healing (see Mt 8:16; Lk 4:39; 13:10–13). His words can change us.

Jesus is the only one who can free the African American woman from the pains of life that may have confined her to a certain position or mindset. Once Jesus touches her life, he brings healing and raises her to a position of servanthood. Then she can serve the needs of others in both her deeds and words. Her gratitude can be seen as she strengthens and encourages other believers by serving them.

—G. London

Reflect on ways Jesus has touched you, lifted you up and spoken to you. Give God thanks by serving others.

Read: Matthew 8:14–15; Mark 1:29–31; Luke 4:38–39.

Hemorrhaging Woman
Faith to Press In

After returning from a trip that took him across the Sea of Galilee, Jesus was surrounded by crowds of people waiting to be healed and to hear him teach. There was a woman in the crowd who had been subject to bleeding for 12 years (see Lk 8:43). Over the years, she had exhausted all of her resources on doctors and medicines, trying to find a cure for her illness, only to be left poor, depressed and sicker than before (see Mk 5:26). She was now considered an untouchable; she was banned from society because she was believed to be "unclean" (see Lev 15:25–30).

When she heard about the man who could heal with just a touch, she believed that he could heal her too. She knew that if she could make it through the crowd and get close enough to touch even the edge of his clothing, she would be made whole. It was her faith in Jesus that gave her the hope that she could be well again. It was her faith in Jesus that made her brave enough to join the crowd, even though she was unclean. When she was able to touch Jesus' cloak, she realized immediately that she had been made well. But, afraid that she might be punished for violating the law of uncleanness, she said nothing.

But Jesus knew who she was and what had happened to him when she touched him, for power had been released from his body at the moment she touched him. He also knew that she needed to overcome her fears and to testify about what had happened to her. He wanted others to know that through faith she was healed and made clean. And he wanted her to know that her faith had healed not only her body, but her soul as well.

—A. Davis

In what area of your life do you need faith to be healed? Use this woman's story to help you press your way to your healing.

Read: Leviticus 15:25–31; Matthew 9:20–22; Mark 5:25–34; Luke 8:43–48.

The Persistent Widow

Always Pray

The parable of the persistent widow reminds us to keep knocking at God's door until we receive an answer. Jesus told this parable to show his followers "that they should always pray and not give up" (Lk 18:1). While the widow in the parable received what she needed from an earthly, unjust judge because she kept asking him to grant her justice, we know that our heavenly Judge is much more just and loving and willing to meet our every need and many of our desires than any earthly judge.

We are to "pray continually" (1Th 5:17). No matter what we are going through or what we need, we must be determined to obtain what we need. Persistence is a virtue. With one thing on our minds, and being very, very persistent, we must do what our widow sister did: wait until our change comes.

When you are in dire need of something, you don't care how far you have to go to get it, how much it's going to cost or what you have to sacrifice in order to get it. A deeply felt need will have you crawling, taking risks and using any means necessary to get it met. In spite of who this widow was, what she was, where she was, she had a need. And she knew where to go to get it met. So, if there's anything you need from Jesus, go to him, look to him. He can be found.

This woman was able to persist because she was doing so based on faith. If no one else knows, certainly African American women know what it's like to be persistent. Our widow sister lets us know that if we pray long and hard enough, God will give us wings as an eagle and feet that won't become weary (see Isa 40:31). "At the proper time we will reap a harvest if we do not give up" (Gal 6:9).

—J. Wharton

Reflect on something you have consistently prayed about. How has God answered your prayers? Look for his work in your life. Be persistent and keep the faith.

Read: Luke 18:1–8.

THE FORGIVEN ADULTERESS

Caught but Not Condemned

She was caught. She was dragged before the men of the community. She was accused. She waited to be stoned—to be destroyed by anything they decided to throw at her.

Had she loved him? Had he told her it would be all right, that he would fix everything, that he loved her? But when the witnesses burst in on them, he apparently didn't protest, didn't defend her and conveniently escaped prosecution. He left her to face her accusers alone. There was nothing she could say that they were willing to hear. The community let him escape, but she would be stoned to death (see Jn 8:3–5).

The guys may have laughed behind their hands when they saw him, but he had his life. On the other hand, all her friends and acquaintances pulled away. After all, she might be after their man. Can't you hear them—her sisters—their words pouring acid into the wound of her shame? There was no one to stand by her side in her defense. Oh, the pain of being the one caught—exposed for the world to see.

You may have tried drugs and were out there for a while. Finally, enough was enough, but now your family doesn't trust you and has trouble believing in you. Your destructive relationships almost cost you your life—black eyes and swollen lips, hospital visits and the inability to hold a job. You are always hiding, afraid and ashamed. You think everyone knows your business and thinks you're unworthy. So, too, our sister must have felt belittled, judged by the self-righteous and found guilty. But out of the crowd, at the point of her deepest fear and need, stepped Jesus!

The Forgiven Adulteress

God is willing to forgive when you repent and turn to him, writing in the dust of your broken life and challenging the finger-pointers to check out the four fingers pointing back at them!

We might be caught, but Jesus does not condemn us! He forgives us! Jesus paid the price for the adulteress and for all of us. Jesus challenges each of us to make new choices; his grace provides both hope for the future and power to leave our sin in the past.

—M. Bellinger

Remember that Jesus does not condemn you as he calls you to leave behind your sin; neither should you condemn yourself or others. With whom can you share this good news today?

Read: Exodus 20:14; Leviticus 20:10; John 7:53—8:11.

Mary and Martha

Grieving Sisters

It is sometimes difficult to believe that death could happen to a sister, brother or someone significant to us. Death, we think, always happens to someone else and at some other time. But all too often death does happen to us and our loved ones at the most unexpected times.

We then begin to realize that the loss of a loved one touches every one of us.

One of the most remarkable and memorable stories in the Bible about family members dealing with death is found in John 11:1–44. It is the story of sisters Mary and Martha and their brother Lazarus. Clearly Jesus had spent some "quality time" with these siblings in Bethany, a town near Jerusalem (see Mk 11:1,11; Lk 10:38–42). When Mary and Martha sent word to Jesus that their brother was sick, they referred to Lazarus as "the one you love" (Jn 11:3).

The powerful lesson in this story is that Mary and Martha became overcomers because they were willing to cast their burdens upon Jesus, which is why they sent for him when Lazarus was dying. When Lazarus died, Jesus comforted them. But he also demonstrated his power to them by raising Lazarus from the dead. It was a miracle that these two sisters had to experience in order to realize the true glory and compassion of Christ (see Jn 11:4,35–36,40).

When you are faced with the difficulty of loss through death or through other means, cast your cares on Jesus. He cares enough to carry your burdens and carry you through your difficult times. Allow him to receive glory from your situation, just as he did from Mary and Martha's.

—D. Moore-James

Mary and Martha

When you have been burdened with the loss of a loved one or when you have been through a challenging situation, to whom have you turned for comfort? What did you receive? Remember to cast your cares on Christ.

Read: John 11:1–44; 1 Peter 5:7.

Mary of Bethany

The Unforgotten Woman

Overwhelmed by the cares of the world, African American women are frequently caring for children, elderly parents or even their extended families.

Mary of Bethany is an example to be followed concerning priorities. She is portrayed as a disciple and a worshiper. As we will see, Jesus commended her actions by declaring that she knew what to choose and that she would not be forgotten.

Mary was often overshadowed by her siblings, Martha and Lazarus—especially by her sister. These sisters represent a duality found within all of us. Sometimes, we see some of Mary's attributes in our lives; at other times, some of Martha's. It is not a matter of good or bad, but rather good and better, concerning our decisions. There are choices and priorities, and hopefully we will make the better choice in a particular situation. We read in Luke 10:38–42 that Jesus affirmed Mary for making the better choice. There would always be tables to set and meals to prepare, but how many opportunities would there be to spend time with the Lord in one's own home?

Seated at the feet of Jesus, Mary was a true disciple. For the first-century Jew, this position symbolized a level of higher education, which was not the norm for women.

Another aspect of Mary's character is that of a worshiper. In John 12:1–3, Mary used costly perfume to anoint Jesus. Jesus said that her action would not be forgotten (see Mt 26:10–13). After being taught by Jesus, Mary seemed to somehow understand that he had to endure the suffering of the cross. Her act of anointing Jesus symbolized his preparation for burial (see Jn 12:7–8). Could she have had a deeper understanding than her male counterparts? As both a disciple and a worshiper, Mary appears to have had the insight or intuition that Jesus would not always be with them. She seized the day and enjoyed being in his presence.

—A. Aubry

How do you seize the day by enjoying God's presence? Walk in his presence throughout this day.

Read: Matthew 26:6–13; Mark 14:1–9; Luke 10:38–42; John 12:1–8.

Sapphira

A Lost Opportunity for Truth

In the early days of the church, individual believers occasionally sold property and voluntarily brought the proceeds to the apostles to be distributed to those in need (see Ac 4:34–37).

During this time, selfishness, a longing for recognition, and deceit entered into the hearts of Sapphira and her husband, Ananias. This couple sold a piece of property and then decided to keep part of the money for themselves and give part of it to the church (see 5:1–2). That would have been fine, but they wanted the apostles and the other believers to think that they were giving all of the money. This couple agreed to lie to the church. In doing so, they ultimately lied to God.

When Sapphira's husband approached the apostles with the money, the Holy Spirit exposed his heart to the apostle Peter. As a result of his evil intent, Ananias died immediately. Three hours later Sapphira arrived, not knowing about her husband's death. God led Peter to question Sapphira, giving her an opportunity to speak truthfully. But Sapphira chose to perpetuate the lie. And, like her husband, this resulted in her immediate death. Sapphira placed more confidence in her husband's evil plan than in God. What could have been a blessing to the church turned into a disaster.

The deaths of Sapphira and her husband shocked the church. God showed them all that he will not tolerate dishonesty in relationships. A woman's relationship with God and her husband should be based on integrity and commitment. She is to respect her husband and agree to godly decisions. She is not told to submit to ungodly or wicked schemes, especially ones that would cause her to be untruthful. It is important for her to keep the marriage covenant—something ordained by God. More important, she is always to keep her covenant with God, never willingly putting herself in a position to break that covenant. If by chance she finds herself faced with an ungodly decision made by her spouse, she should speak the truth in love so they can grow together spiritually.

—G. London

How has not telling the entire truth hurt you in the past? Seek to live life truthfully—before God, others and yourself.

Read: Acts 4:32—5:11; Ephesians 4:14–15,25.

Candace
Secure Leader

Just as "Pharaoh" was a reference to the king of Egypt, "Candace" was the title given to the queen of Ethiopia (see Ac 8:27). This queen was perhaps a successor to the queen of Sheba (see 1Ki 10:1). As a ruler in Ethiopia (not the area known as modern Ethiopia, but an area in what is now southern Egypt and northern Sudan), Candace led one of the oldest African nations.

A eunuch, the finance chairman of Candace's treasury and obviously a person who was attracted to Judaism, had gone to Jerusalem to worship. As he was returning home, he sat in his chariot, reading and trying to understand the writings of the prophet Isaiah. Philip, a Christian believer led by the Spirit of God, came along and explained to him the Scriptures and the good news about Jesus.

The fact that this man was allowed to go to Jerusalem to worship speaks volumes about Candace's leadership. The eunuch's understanding of the Scriptures was paramount to his ability to manage the financial affairs of the queen. With greater understanding, he could put his Lord, his life and his job in the proper perspective. The queen benefited from the spirituality of her finance chairman. Believing in God enabled him to deal fairly with others and thus enhance the integrity of her kingdom. As a result of this faith, the eunuch could be long-suffering and kind to those he met. It is quite possible that his strong faith and beliefs were qualities the queen recognized and applauded. She possibly looked beyond his managerial capabilities to his heart, and she found a man compassionate and loving. She sought and found an individual whom she could trust because he worked to please God first and others second.

Candace was confident in who she was, so she did not feel threatened by the eunuch's service to someone else. Because of her confidence, it's likely safe to say that many in the area of ancient Ethiopia and beyond know Christ today. Imagine what would have happened if she had not been a confident leader; she may have tried to suppress her treasurer. The story then would have turned out much differently.

—J. Chambers

How can you incorporate characteristics of Candace's secure leadership into your life? Remember that when you are secure, you have no need to hurt others.

Read: Acts 8:26–39.

Rhoda
Doing Her Duty

Rhoda was a servant girl in the household of Mary the mother of John Mark. It was in Mary's home that the believers gathered to pray for the release of Peter. That night Rhoda was doing her duty. She could have been complaining about being a servant and not being able to participate in the prayer meeting. She could have been preoccupied with her own thoughts and not attending to her task. She could have even wandered off to her own devices—for after all, although a group was assembled, their eyes were probably closed!

But Rhoda was doing her duty. She was listening for sounds beyond the door so she could warn those gathered of impending danger. The group's prayer was for Peter's safety, for he had again been taken to prison for his courageous preaching.

During the prayer session, Rhoda heard a knock at the

door (see Ac 12:13). She recognized Peter's voice and immediately told those praying that their prayers had been answered. Those praying did not believe her (see Ac 12:15). They told her that the knocking must have been done by Peter's angel. But Rhoda never doubted that it was Peter's voice that she heard. She knew that God had heard and answered their prayers.

We can follow Rhoda's example of simple, childlike faith. In the face of others' disbelief, we can stand strong and keep believing. God will answer our prayers in his own way. We must be prepared and ready to receive his answer.

—E. Watson

How are you preparing to receive God's answer to your prayers?

Read: Acts 12:1–19.

LYDIA
A Model for Women in Business

Lydia was a fascinating woman. A successful businesswoman, she traded in dye and dyed goods. Purple cloth was her specialty—a color of fabric that few could afford. She probably had a love for texture and design, and her creative side was balanced with a good sense for business.

Lydia was not only a successful and noted businesswoman, she was also a worshiper of God. On the Sabbath, Lydia was with a group of women by the bank of the river. When she heard Paul's message about Christ, she became a believer and was baptized (see Ac 16:13–15).

Lydia was also a woman of great influence. Her entire household was baptized after she opened her heart to Paul's message. She also felt compelled to invite Paul and his companions into her home. Lydia obviously impressed Paul and the others with her strong leadership. They accepted her invitation to stay with her.

Lydia receives only brief recognition in the book of Acts, yet she symbolizes the importance of strong and capable women in the church's earliest history. She was the first recorded Gentile convert in Europe, one of the first known Christian businesswomen and one of the first believers to open her home for Christian service. She took care of her business as well as God's business.

Women were converts to Christ from the start. From the beginning of church history, women publicly declared themselves followers of Jesus. Even while the disciples were in hiding, it was to women that the risen Christ was first revealed. Women were the ones who searched out the men to bring them the good news of Jesus' resurrection, and women like Lydia helped to support the spread of the Good News.

—R. Walker

What are you doing to help share the Good News of Christ with others?

Read: Acts 16:6–15, 40.

Fortune-Telling Slave Girl
A Surprising Testimony to God's Work

Fortune-telling was a common practice in the Greek and Roman cultures in New Testament times. Divination, the attempt to foretell the unknown and predict the future, and many superstitious practices were common. In the Jewish culture these practices were punishable by death (see Lev 20:27; Dt 18:10–12). Those who practiced fortune-telling were astrologers, charmers, false prophets and sorcerers.

A young slave girl possessed with a spirit of divination approached Paul and Silas one day when they went to preach at Philippi (see Ac 16:16). The demonic spirit gave her the power to predict the future. The spirit spoke the truth mockingly. Her masters profited from her unfortunate condition by using her for their own gain.

She followed Paul and Silas for several days, yelling that these men were servants of the Most High God and were showing the people the way of salvation (see Ac 16:17). Being grieved in his spirit, Paul took spiritual authority over the unclean spirit and commanded it to leave the young girl. In the name of Jesus, the girl was freed. Her owners were angry when they realized that any chance of making more money from the slave girl was gone. As a result, Paul and Silas were taken before the magistrates, beaten, imprisoned and carefully watched by the prison guard. Through prayer and singing, the miraculous occurred. An earthquake shook the prison doors open, and the prisoners' chains came loose. Grateful that the prisoners did not escape and that he was stopped from committing suicide by Paul, the guard—along with his entire family—was saved and baptized.

This is the only time the book of Acts mentions the fortune-telling slave girl. Her testimony, however, will stand forever, proving that God can bring glory out of the most unfair, abusive and harsh situations. In today's society, divination is subtly camouflaged as entertainment. The commercials and infomercials are creative enough to raise a woman's curiosity. The most important areas of life are targeted: love, sex and work. Women of color must be careful not to fall prey to demonic spirits. We must trust in the true God for our future because his voice is truth.

—G. London

Whose voice do you listen to regarding the plans for your future?

Read: Acts 16:16–40.

Philip's Daughters
Those Preaching Women

In the world of the Bible, women were often mentioned in passing, if at all. Yet their gifts and contributions to the life of the community and the work of the ministry often shine through like a candle in a dark room. Such is the case with the daughters of Philip. Acts 21:9 makes a cursory reference to these women. As a matter of fact, one could read this chapter and completely overlook the significance of these women's ministries.

Philip had four daughters (no mention is made of his wife). They were women of high moral character who apparently had chosen to be single and celibate. They were preaching women—women who spoke inspired utterances from God. And they were appreciated for more than their prophetic gifts. A couple of centuries later, the church historian Eusebius wrote that Philip's daughters were recognized as authorities on persons and events of the early church. In fact, Philip and his daughters may well have been key information sources for Luke, the author of the Gospel of Luke and the book of Acts. Yet they lived in a culture that typically denied the personhood and presence of women.

Historical as well as contemporary African American women have faced a similar situation. Too often our contributions have been overlooked in the light of the achievements of African American men. Yet the powerful public preaching of women such as Jarena Lee, Florence Spearing Randolph and Vashti McKenzie continue to break through. As a community of believers, we must work together as women and men of God in the spread of the gospel. Supportive of the gifts that we each bring to the task, we are to model inclusion, thereby advancing God's kingdom.

Whether you are called by God to preach the gospel from the pulpit or to serve faithfully in the pew, as a woman, you continue to play a significant role in the church, in society and in the advancement of God's kingdom. We cannot allow culture, tradition, denomination or gender to hinder us from that which God has called and anointed us to do. Black women: Preach on!

—E. Crawford

What has God called you to do today? Do it faithfully!

Read: Joel 2:28–29; Matthew 19:10–12; Acts 21:8–9; 1 Corinthians 7:32–35.

Phoebe

A Faithful Messenger

Phoebe, like other women in both the early church and the church today, sacrificed countless hours for the advancement of God's kingdom through her various church ministries (see Ro 16:1–2).

She remained focused on the goal of spreading the Good News and accomplished this task against insurmountable odds. Driven by her deep sense of desire, purpose, faith and commitment, Phoebe traveled many miles in order to deliver the apostle Paul's letter to the Christians at Rome. This letter was important, for its contents would become the bridge to understanding God's plan for future Christians. Phoebe's steadfast motivation touched the hearts of countless people who otherwise may not have been receptive to the gospel. Without this diligent and faithful servant, we might not have the book of Romans from which to read and garner spiritual insight.

Phoebe goes virtually unnoticed in the Biblical text, and many servants of Christ today—especially women of color—go unnoticed too. However, Phoebe's work was very important. In Romans 16:1, Paul called her a "servant of the church in Cenchrea." Used in this way, the word "servant" probably refers to the position of woman deacon, or deaconess (see NIV text note on Ro 16:1). She served those who were receiving the message of salvation, and she carried that message to others. While our work may be trying at times, we must focus on the outcome. Others will be blessed in ways we cannot foresee. It is natural to want recognition and affirmation for our work; however, we must not lose focus when we are not acknowledged. Our true Rewarder sees our hard work and knows what we do. Phoebe serves as an example of a faithful servant who is empowered by God to serve.

Women of color, work as servants to God; glorify God through all your tasks, and he will remember you as a faithful servant. He will receive the glory, and you and others will be blessed.

—K. Davis

How can you adopt an attitude as a servant of God in all you do today?

Read: Romans 16:1–2.

Priscilla

An Open-Door Policy

Priscilla was a bold and courageous woman who met the apostle Paul in Corinth. Like Paul, Priscilla and her husband, Aquila, were tentmakers.

Pricilla and Aquila opened their home to Paul, and they became partners with him both in business and in the ministry of the gospel (see Ac 18:1–3). Priscilla wore a familiar crown to women of color: She was not afraid to speak and stand up for what she believed in. Without ever elevating herself above others, she faithfully took her instructions from the Lord and served others; the gospel was taken further because of her.

Priscilla was loyal and devoted. Priscilla and Aquila labored for the gospel as a team. Their names are always mentioned together when they are referred to in the New Testament (see Ac 18:2,18–19,26; Ro 16:3; 1Co 16:19; 2Ti 4:19). What is even more unusual is that Priscilla is generally mentioned first—a hint that she may have played a more active role in ministry than did her husband.

When Paul left Corinth, he took Priscilla and Aquila with him. He left the couple at Ephesus to lay the groundwork for what would become one of the most important churches of the New Testament period (see Ac 18:18–21). During that time Apollos, who would become an influential preacher and leader in the church (see 1Co 1:12; 3:1–7), humbled himself and sat at Priscilla and Aquila's feet to receive instruction (see Ac 18:24–28). Apollos knew and taught only John the Baptist's baptism. Priscilla could have found fault in him, but instead she helped him. She and her husband invited Apollos to their home and compassionately shared the complete gospel message with him. Apollos may not have been able to understand that Jesus was the Savior and then convince his fellow Jews of this truth if it had not been for Priscilla.

Just like so many women who are full of love, wisdom and courage, Priscilla remained a witness and a student of the gospel. She worked side by side with her husband, spreading the Word while also managing her business, church and home.

—W. Johnson

How does Priscilla inspire you to be a student of the Word and to use your gifts and your home in Christ's service?

Read: Acts 18; Romans 16:3–5; 1 Corinthians 16:19.

Euodia and Syntyche

Women in Conflict

The apostle Paul held Euodia and Syntyche in high esteem.

He glowingly referred to them as "women who have contended at my side in the cause of the gospel" (Php 4:3). However, we find Paul addressing the conduct of these two women in his letter to the Philippians—a letter meant to be read to the church publicly no less! Euodia and Syntyche were feuding about some matter that could ultimately have disrupted the life of the church. Therefore, Paul asked the saints in general and an unnamed third person in particular—Paul's "loyal yokefellow" (Php 4:3; see the NIV text note)—to work at bringing about reconciliation between these two women.

Euodia and Syntyche were truly an asset to Paul's ministry. They contributed greatly to the local church, which is why Paul was adamant about bringing wholeness and healing to this situation. If left unchecked, this conflict could have caused harm to both him and the church. When there is division in the household of faith, the work of the church is hindered. Whatever the issue was between Euodia and Syntyche, Paul wanted to put it to rest, and he wanted the other believers to assist in making that happen.

As women of color and of faith, we must focus on important matters and not dwell on minor issues. The time we waste arguing about insignificant matters could be better used doing something to advance the work of the Lord.

Instead of feuding, Paul encourages the saints to rejoice and be gentle with one another (see Php 4:4–5). How can we attract others to the church if we are at odds with each other? They see enough of that outside the church. While we may not always agree with one another, we can strive to compromise. Things do not always have to go our way. We must remember that everyone is someone important to Christ. When we understand this, we will respect each other.

When we are rejoicing in the Lord, we will find ways to encourage someone else. We will consider the other person's well-being just as we would our own. Strife and division are tools of our adversary, so we must continue to focus on our goal: to glorify God and help others live fulfilled lives in Christ.

—D. Stroman

Is there a woman of faith you need to reconcile with or others you need to help reconcile? Pray for guidance in your situation.

Read: Philippians 2:1–11; 4:2–9.

Claudia

A Sincere Supporter

One story that was told to me when I was child has meant more to me as an adult than when I first heard it. That story focused on a woman who had three daughters.

Each daughter was considered a valuable member of society: a prominent physician, a leading criminal attorney and a renowned vocalist. Life provided its challenges to each daughter. There were times when they doubted themselves, their abilities to handle situations and their understanding of what their system taught. Yet these women had a praying mother, grandmother, aunt, niece or daughter who was always available to offer encouragement or who never stopped praying.

Everyone needs a cheering squad and a support base. As women of color, we can appreciate the value of stored prayers and those who keep the faith in our stead. Claudia was such an ambassador to young Timothy and Paul (see 2Ti 4:21).

We don't know much about Claudia, but she is mentioned by Paul as a member of Paul's circle of supporters. She must have been the type of person who supported her leader despite what others thought. She was an encourager, nurturer and strong supporter. I believe that the reason Claudia was so supportive is that she did not put her total trust in the messenger, but in the message. Faith was the key to her maintaining a positive base and supportive spirit. She understood the message of Christ; she knew him and what he had done for her and what he promised to do for all believers. Therefore, she was able to support others who were ambassadors for Christ.

Claudia could have been our great-grandmother, grandmother or mother who prevailed through many tribulations and whose travails continue. Despite it all, our Claudias continue to look toward the hills for their help (see Ps 121). That's how they are able to be supportive prayer warriors.

—B. Kitt

Reflect on the women who have constantly prayed for you and served as your support base. How can you be a support to other women?

Read: John 17:20–23; 2 Timothy 4:21.

The "Chosen Lady"

A Woman Worth Imitating

There is some debate whether the "chosen lady" of 2 John is a literal or figurative woman.

Taken literally, the epistle is written to a particular woman and her children. Taken figuratively, it refers to a local church and its members. Whether a local church or one special woman, the "chosen lady" is to be emulated. This priceless narrative exemplifies what it means to live, love, walk and serve in the spirit of truth. The recipient of this letter enjoyed saintly character and distinguished privilege.

John commended the chosen lady for her virtue and the religious education of her children, and he exhorted her to remain in the doctrine of Christ, to preserve the truth and to carefully avoid the delusions of false teachers. John also commends her and her children for remaining faithful to the truth of the gospel, and he urged them to obey the command to love one another. "As you have heard from the beginning, his command is that you walk in love" (2Jn 6).

At this time in the history of the early church, there were many dangerous false teachers who twisted the truth. John encouraged the woman not to take in perpetrators; instead, she was to practice the great commandment of Christian love and charity while being aware of deceivers. As Jesus said, this woman was to be as shrewd as a snake and as innocent as a dove (see Mt 10:16).

Others loved this lady too, not for her rank but for her holiness. She was not only a chosen one, but also a choice one—a woman of refinement and good manners. She was also honest and treated people with integrity.

The "ChosenLady"

We are to emulate this chosen lady. Whether or not we are actual leaders in our church, we need to be women of virtue to build our church and communities from the inside out. We are the church, so it is imperative that we are included as role models.

—P. George

How are you walking in love? Follow the chosen lady's example today.

Read: 2 John.

THE REVELATION 12 WOMAN

A Woman of Focus

Picture this woman. She was pregnant and seemingly alone and in pain as she anticipated the birth of her child. Suddenly, her worst enemy appeared.

His breath was on her. He waited to devour the baby as soon as it appeared. How he hated her! He could have easily killed them both immediately. But no, he wanted her to see her child die.

In extreme peril, the woman delivered the boy. Before the enemy could snatch him, the child was swept up to God. Still weak from the birth experience, the woman rose to her feet and ran. With unstable hips and wobbly legs, she ran for her life.

She spoke to no one. She never pleaded with the enemy nor did she call for help. She ran, even without her baby, to the place God had prepared. And the devil followed.

Michael and the angels fought the enemy, and he was hurled from heaven. Still he tried to kill the woman. But God gave the woman the wings of an eagle to speed her escape. Then the serpent sprayed out water from his mouth, but the earth swallowed the flood, allowing the woman another escape. At this point, the devil, defeated and still hating the woman, dedicated his life to killing her earthbound seed.

Who was this woman? We do not know for sure, but she is obviously symbolic and her attributes are instructive. She was strong, courageous—clearly a soldier. The woman had been given specific instruction. She understood what she was to do. Once on her mission, she executed it without question or complaint. Her circumstances and her feelings were irrelevant. Help came from unexpected places. Her success depended on her staying in action—no matter what. Timing was everything.

The Revelation 12 woman was a woman of focus. Self-sacrifice was just the beginning of the contribution she made to life. She gave all she had; the enemy couldn't stop her, and heaven and earth moved on her behalf. She knew her help was in God, and his plans were fulfilled.

—V. Hartsfield

How focused are you on carrying out the mission of God? Use this woman's strength and determination to encourage you as you run your race.

Read: 1 Corinthians 9:24–25; Hebrews 12:1–3; Revelation 12.

Contributors to the Original
Women of Color Study Bible

Marjorie Lawson - General Editor
Rev. Estrelda Alexander
Professor Linda L. Ammons
Dr. Pamela June Anderson
Rev. Chestina Archibald
Mrs. Marcia B Armstead
Rev. Angela D. Aubry
Rev. Lisa Miller Autry
Rev. Karen E. Mosby-Avery
Rev. Mary Anne Allen Bellinger
Rev. Cynthia B. Belt
Ms. Keya Belt
Ms. Jetola Anderson-Blair
Rev. Winfred Blagmond
Rev. Michele Cotton Bohanon
Rev. Toni R. Booker
Dr. Ann Bouie
Rev. Cookie Frances Lee Bracey
Rev. Nina Bryant

Rev. Marion Wyvetta Bullock
Attorney Candace Lorelle Byrd
Minister Terri L. Byrd
Rev. Lajuana D. Caldwell
Dr. Iva Carruthers
Rev. Jacquetta Chambers
Rev. Monica Anita Coleman
Dr. Suzan D. Johnson Cook
Rev. Charmayne Cooke
Rev. Maria-Alma Rainey Copeland
Dr. A. Elaine Crawford
Rev. Alice J. Burnette Davis
Rev. Katherine J. Davis
Rev. Sandra Debby
Rev. Alice Dise
Rev. Troy Janel Harrison-Dixon
Rev. Lasandra Melton-Dolberry
Rev. Marcia L. Dyson
Dr. Violet Lucinda Fisher
Dr. Leah Gaskin Fitchue
Dr. Margaret Elaine McCollins Flake
Dr. Abena Safiyah Fosua
Rev. Beverly Jackson Garvin
Ms. Portia George

Ms. Sha Givens

Dr. Arlene W, Gordon

Dr. Cynthia Hale

Rev. Cecilia Swafford Harris

Mrs. Hattie G. Harris

Ms. Vanessa Hartsfield

Rev. Kellie V. Hayes

Rev. Raye Evelyn Haynes

Rev. Barbara Ann Heard

Ms. Kelly Hill

Dr. Lottie Jones Hood

Dr. Janet Hopkins

Ms. Arnesa A. Howell

Rev. Darlene Moore-James

Rev. Deborah L. Shumake Japhia

Dr. Diane Johnson

Rev. Frankye Anthea Sourie Johnson

Rev. Katurah Worrill Johnson

Rev. Wilma R. Johnson

Rev. Jolene Josey

Mrs. Marjorie L. Kimbrough

Rev. Bonita A. Kitt

Marjorie Lawson

Dr. Linda Lee

Rev. Ginger D. London

Dr. Carolyn B. Love

Ms. Victoria Lowe

Mrs. Dinah Page Mannes

Mrs. Ann Shenthia Manuel

Dr. Delores E. Lee McCabe

Chaplain Emma Louise McNair

Rev. Bernadine Grant McRipley

Rev. Andrea L. Middleton

Dr. Ella Pearson Mitchell

Dr. Sherry Davis Molock

Evangelist Alberiene Riene Adams-Morris

Ms. Victoria Christopher Murray

Rev. Naomi Peete

Rev. Anita Adams Powell

Ms. Constance Richards

Ms. Shewanda Riley

Rev. Monique Robinson

Rev. Sheila Ford Robinson

Rev. Jannah Scott

Rev. Angela Stewart Sims

Dr. Kathyrn R. Smallwood

Minister Terri McFaddin-Solomon
Dr. Malvina V. Stephens
Rev. Dorothea J. Belt Stroman
Rev. Deborah Tinsley Taylor
Rev. Meriann Taylor
Rev. Jacqueline Thompson
Dr. La Verne Tolbert
Togetta S. Ulmer
Rev. Tanya S. Wade
Rev. N.S. "Robin" Walker
Rev. Elaine P. Walters
Rev. Cheryl D. Ward
Minister Katara A. Washington-Patton
Dr. Elizabeth D. Watson
Rev. Joan C. Webster
Dr. Joan L. Wharton
Rev. Barbara J. Whipple
Rev. Bessie Whitaker
Dr. Leah Elizabeth Mosley White
Dr. Bernadette Glover-Williams
Rev. Mary Newbern-Williams
Yolanda Williams
Rev. Portia Turner Williamson

Ms. Cheryl Wilson
Rev. Jane E. Wood
Rev. Lois A. Wooden
Rev. Cynthia E. Woods
Mrs. Beverly Yates

$49.99
ISBN 978-1-958779-04-0

WOMEN of COLOR
STUDY BIBLE

KING JAMES
VERSION

$69.99
ISBN 978-1-958779-06-4

It's going to be a God Hair Day!

by Mel Banks II
ILLUSTRATED BY LAWRENCE PAUL-OKOH

ISBN 978-1-958779-08-8

$8.99

LARGE PRINT
WORKBOOK
& PERSONAL
STUDY GUIDE

EQUIPPED
FOR SMALL AND LARGE GROUPS

WOMEN OF THE BIBLE FOR
Women of Color

$16.99
ISBN 979-8-9853690-7-6

☑ GOALS

Become an US Urban Spirit! Publishing and Media Company Independent or Church Distributor Today!

- earn extra money
- engage with more people
- change lives
- join a winning team
- distribute high-quality Bibles and books

Go to www.urbanspirit.biz

Order your Independent or Church Distributor "Starter Kit" today online. It contains everything you need to get started selling right away.
Or call **800.560.1690** to get started today!

Notes

Notes

Notes

Notes

Notes

Notes

Notes

Notes

Notes